The Original
Betty's Pies
Favorite
RECIPES

Betty's Pies

by Betty Lessard

Lake Superior
Port Cities Inc.

First Edition: June 2001

10 9 8 7 6

LAKE SUPERIOR PORT CITIES INC.
P.O. Box 16417
Duluth, Minnesota 55816-0417 USA
1-888-BIG LAKE (888-244-5253) • www.lakesuperior.com
Publishers of *Lake Superior Magazine* and *Lake Superior Travel Guide*

Library of Congress Cataloging-In-Publication Data

Lessard, Betty, 1924-
   Betty's Pies favorite recipes / Betty Lessard. – 1st ed.
       p. cm.
   Includes index.
   ISBN 0-942235-50-9
   ISBN 978-0-942235-50-0
   1. Betty's Pies (Bakery). 2. Pies. I. Title
   TX773 .L4625 2001
   641.8'652 - dc21   2001029835

Printed in Canada

   Design: Matt Pawlak, Erica Nord
   Editors: Paul L. Hayden, Hugh E. Bishop, Konnie LeMay
   Printing: Friesens Book Division, Winnipeg, Manitoba

Dedication

For my parents, Aleck and Minnie Christiansen,
without whom none of this could have happened.
Dedicated also to Lloyd, my husband and best friend,
who helped me in so many ways.

Acknowledgments

I have so many folks to thank for the many contributions they have all made, for the recipes they have shared, the help in getting this book together and all my customers who made the whole thing possible.

A special thanks to my sister, Karen Storms, and friends Leigh Elking and Jean Erwin who helped in the writing of the history.

I also want to remember my special friend of 20 years, June Heurlin, who kept after me all those years to get to work on this book. She passed away on December 30, 2000, but did have her input into this book. It is too bad that she couldn't see her dream come true.

A big thanks to Carl and Marti (the new owners of Betty's Pies) for bringing Betty's Pies back to where it was when I left in 1984. I will continue to work with them and assist them whenever they need me. It is always good to go over there and greet former customers. Last week, as I was leaving Betty's, a customer greeted me. He remembered me from the '60s and reminded me of things that I had on the menu at that time, like the Frozen Fruit Salad with the pineapple dressing that was his favorite.

A note of appreciation to Laura Zahn, a well-published cookbook author who read the manuscript. A few of the gals who cooked for me during some of those years also deserve a lot of credit – Lori, Toni and Peggy. Steve, my nephew, also did cooking. He enjoys cooking today. Also, a big thanks for all the gals and fellows who have worked for me during the 28 years I was in business.

Table of Contents

The Original Betty's
In the Beginning

My family, the Christiansens, were in the wholesale fish business in Duluth, Minnesota, buying fish along Lake Superior's Minnesota north shore and at Isle Royale, processing the fish in Duluth and shipping their products all over the country.

The business, H. Christiansen and Sons, was named for my Grandfather Hans, who arrived in the Hayward, Wisconsin, area from the Lofoten Islands of Norway in 1879. He moved the family to Duluth in 1888 and fished Lake Superior in the summertime from a camp at Crow Creek and in the harbor off of Park Point in Duluth during the winter. He and my uncle, Captain Martin, with my father Aleck and Uncle Otto, started the family fish business in Duluth in 1898.

Headquarters for H. Christiansen and Sons was behind the Marshall-Wells Building in Duluth, Minnesota. During the 1930s, the *Winyah* would pull up several times a week to unload its cargo of fish. Duluth's famed Aerial Bridge is in the background.

At that time, there was no highway along the north shore and all the fish were transported by boat. The company dock and building were just inside Duluth Harbor near the Aerial Lift Bridge (actually, it was an aerial car ferry back then) behind what is Grandma's Marketplace in Canal Park today. They sold fresh, salted and smoked fish and would sell canned spiced fish products under the Hogstad Fish Company label. They also manufactured nets and other equipment that the fishermen needed, as well as investing in other business interests.

The first boat the family operated was called the *Grace J.,* followed by the *Hazel* (named after their youngest sister). In 1924, they purchased the *Winyah,* which had been built in 1894 as Andrew Carnegie's yacht. After the purchase, the 115-foot boat was stripped of most of its yachting finery and converted by Marine Iron and Shipbuilding Company of Duluth to carry 74 tons of fish, freight and up to 22 passengers.

As a child, I would beg my mother to take my brother and me down to see the *Winyah* leave on Saturday mornings. I must admit that the main reason I wanted to go was because Uncle Martin would always slip each of us kids a 50-cent piece.

I also remember my aunt telling me about spending summers with my grandma at the family's cabin by the Stewart River. My uncle would bring supplies to them on the *Winyah.* He'd anchor just offshore and blow the whistle. My aunt would rush down to the river, hop into a little boat and row out to the *Winyah* for their supplies. Many times the sea was so rough that my aunt wondered if she would make it back to shore. My uncle would wait until he could see that she was safely into the river before going full steam ahead to his next stop.

After the SS *America* sank at Isle Royale in 1928 and the Booth Fisheries Company decided to end its Duluth operations, H. Christiansen & Sons took over the bulk of the north shore fish business. The *Winyah* remained the primary boat serving fishermen on the north shore, but especially those at Isle Royale – since water transportation of fish decreased after Highway 61 opened in 1924-25 and truckers started hauling fish from the north shore to Duluth. Without that land transportation option, Isle Royale

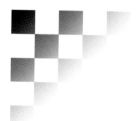

During the 1920s, H. Christiansen and Sons conducted business in a tin shed behind the Marshall-Wells Building in Duluth. Here, Captain Martin Christiansen (left), his brother Aleck (Betty's father) and bookkeeper Gene Dunphy (right) pose for the camera.

fishermen remained dependent on the Christiansen fish boats right to the time that fishing drastically decreased in the 1950s because of the lamprey.

The *Winyah* became one of the most famous boats operating here, departing from Duluth with 30 tons of ice for the fishermen to pack fish in and returning with the catch from hundreds of fishermen scattered along its route. A round trip between Isle Royale and Duluth took two days and nights, with many stops at secluded locations to pick up 100-pound boxes and kegs of fish from the fishermen, who received seven cents a pound in the early 1930s. Even as late as 1944, one historian states that the company processed 6 million pounds of fish per season.[1]

The fishermen would also give the captain their orders for groceries and any other items that they needed and he would fill their orders and bring them on the next trip the boat would make, which was twice a week.

Of all the freight the boat hauled through its years of service, probably the most unusual was the occasional cow that a fisherman would buy and need delivered to his homestead. The *Winyah*'s crew would maneuver the boat as near shore as possible, force the cow into the water and she'd have to swim to shore with the fisherman either leading or chasing her in his skiff.

The boat would begin the Isle Royale run in early April and tie up for the season in late November. With its steel hull, the *Winyah* was often the first ship to leave Duluth in the spring, breaking ice on its way out.

[1]Nute, Grace Lee, *Lake Superior*, Bobbs-Merrill Company, New York City, 1944, pp.187-191.

Likewise, in the fall, it often made the last trip of the year through ice fields to get winter supplies to the fishermen and bring in one last load of fish. In the years before rail and truck service on the north shore, that last trip of the fish boat was critical, since it often carried all the supplies the fishermen would need for the winter months ahead, when they were completely isolated at their homesteads for several months. For a few years, some fishermen and their families stayed on Isle Royale all winter. Imagine how they must have looked forward to the first signs of spring, when the *Winyah* would arrive with their mail and a supply of groceries.

The boxes of iced fish being picked up would be brought to Duluth to be processed and sold to local restaurants or shipped throughout the country. In late fall, when the herring run was on, the workers at the company would put in long hours filleting and salting down the herring and packing them into boxes, load railroad boxcars and send them off to Chicago and other major cities.

In 1943, there were 240 commercial fishermen along the north shore between Duluth and Grand Marais, including Isle Royale. They produced millions of pounds of fish, but those days are long gone. Today there are only about 30 commercial and apprentice licenses issued in the entire area from Duluth to the Canadian border.

The original smoked fish shack catered to customers who walked up to a window to order. Around 1955, the first of five expansions allowed them to order from inside the building.

In 1939, Uncle Martin died and my dad and Uncle Otto took over management of the company. By the time of his death, the family business was involved in a number of companies, including H. Christiansen & Sons, Hogstad Fish Company, Duluth-Chicago Freight Lines and Marine Iron and Shipbuilding. Upon his death, Andy Jorgenson, who had worked for the family for several years, became captain of the *Winyah*.

During World War II, the family sold the *Winyah* because it required quite a large crew. Walter Bowe, president of The Aggregates Company of Duluth, bought the boat and used it in his gravel business for a few years, then removed the cabin and used it as part of his lake cottage. He sold the *Winyah* to Leonard Rosen of Union Compressed Steel Company. It is assumed that the boat ended up being scrapped by that company.

The family bought the *Detroit*, a smaller diesel-powered boat, to replace the *Winyah*. The *Detroit* made the run from Grand Marais to Isle Royale in just a few hours. Captain Andy and my father did this run and Dad would then deliver the fish by truck into Duluth for processing and distribution. This was possible because Highway 61 had been improved and Dad drove from Duluth to Grand Marais twice a week, while Andy lived on the boat.

When my dad was in Duluth, he would fill grocery orders for the fishermen and pick up whatever else they needed. Can you imagine grocery shopping for more than 25 families at one time, compiling the almost illegible lists written on scraps of paper, then separating the individual orders so each family received only their own supplies?

One time when my dad was checking out at the grocery store, he paid the bill, went out to the car and discovered a stray ketchup bottle in his pocket. He looked up to find the clerks standing at the window watching him and laughing as he held up the ketchup bottle. When he went back in to pay for it, they said they were wondering how long it would take before he realized he had it. They knew he had it all the time and it had already been added to the bill.

This continued for several years. In the spring of 1951, my brother, Alan, joined the company. Unfortunately in June of that year, on the way back from Grand Marais, Dad had an unavoidable accident and my brother was killed instantly. That took the wind out of Dad's sails. His heart was no longer in running the boat. The next year he put it up for sale.

In 1953, after the sale of the *Detroit*, Captain Andy was out of work and, since he had no family, my dad put an 8-by-8-foot fish stand on the property that had been owned by the family at Stewart River since 1909. Dad asked Andy to run it so that he'd have something to do. It was called Andy's Smoked Fish Shack and I remember feeling sorry for Andy, sitting there by the hour waiting for customers. Little did I know that I would be the one waiting for customers in a year or two.

After three years of tending the stand, Captain Andy passed away and Dad asked me if I wanted to take over. I said I'd try it for a couple of weeks to see how I liked it. Twenty-eight years later I was still there, so I guess I liked it pretty well.

My husband, Lloyd, and I were living in Duluth at the time. Lloyd worked for Minnesota Power, so I would drop him off at work, then drive to Two Harbors every day to run the fish stand. My father would pick Lloyd up after work and bring him up to the fish stand. My mother would drive up if I needed extra help. We did this until 1959, when we built homes near the fish stand, which was now called "Betty's."

It didn't take me long to figure out that I needed to offer more than just the smoked fish and crackers served on wrapping paper, so I added donuts and coffee and soon bought a small used grill so I could make hamburgers. We had an old-fashioned hand pump on the hill behind the stand. We had to pump the water, carry it down the hill and heat it on a small gas grill. Later that summer we put in an electrical pump so we had cold running water.

We used disposable cups, which Lloyd took to the dump every night, but he kept saying that we were just throwing money away every trip, so our next step was to purchase china cups and silverware. Later in the summer, we again expanded our menu, adding hot dogs.

When I found some spare time, I began doing some baking, but found that the little fish stand was getting pretty cramped. It was time to add on to the building – the first of five additions. In addition to needing more kitchen space, we wanted a place for people to come in and sit down to eat their smoked fish or hamburgers and hot dogs, so we added a lunch counter. After a couple of years there was such a drop in smoked fish sales that we decided to discontinue handling it and specialize in fresh trout dinners,

because I could get fresh trout nearly every day. At this time we changed the name to "Betty's Cafe" and I began doing much more baking.

Reserve Mining Company's taconite plant in Silver Bay opened in 1955 and many workers drove daily from Two Harbors and Duluth. They began stopping in for pie and coffee on their way home from work. At that time, fresh strawberry pie was 30 cents a slice and 5 cents extra for whipped cream. I would try out new pie recipes on these fellows at no cost to them. They would tell me if I should keep making the recipe or change it. They were my excellent taste testers.

In 1958, we decided to build our home next to the restaurant. My folks built their house first and we built ours next door to them. My dad and Lloyd still drove into Duluth every day to work. My mother would help me in the restaurant during the day. Until Lloyd passed away in 1975, he was always there to help on weekends.

My folks would spend Saturday afternoons sitting in the back corner of the restaurant cleaning at least six crates of strawberries for me to use the next day in my pies. My dad would then go out and take care of other chores around the place. If we got busy and needed help we would hang an apron out the back door and he would come to the rescue. We did this many times.

The second big expansion to Betty's Cafe came at the end of the 1950s when indoor seating at a counter was added.

7

In the early days of the smelting season, people were everywhere. Cars lined the roads and folks caught naps wherever they could find room. The smelt run also meant pulling all-nighters at Betty's to protect the property from wood-snatching firemakers.

At about that same time, smelting became popular. Smelt are a small fish, bigger than a sardine and smaller than a herring. In the spring when the water reaches a certain temperature, they swim up the rivers at night to spawn. In those days, there were so many smelt that people would line the banks with long-handled dip nets and wade out, dip their nets into the river or lake and catch dozens of smelt with each dip. They came from all over: North and South Dakota, most of Minnesota and a large area south into Wisconsin.

At night, temperatures were typically below freezing. The dip nets would freeze instantly when taken out of the icy water. The smelters made fires all along the riverbanks to keep warm in the raw windy spring nights. We had always closed the restaurant at night, but found that the smelters would take any wood they could find for their fires. One night we lost the roof of our pump house, another night our front porch was gone and one time we caught some guys trying to take our flower boxes.

We decided we'd better stay open all night on weekends during smelting season to protect our property. My Dad and Lloyd would keep the restaurant open until 5 a.m., when I would come in and take over. Many nights the smelters would come into the restaurant and lay their frozen mitts on our heater to thaw them out while they had a cup of coffee or a piece of pie. My dad and the fire warden, Harold Koop, patrolled the area to be sure the fires were under control.

I often wonder what the families must have thought of the odors that lingered in the smelters' cars after they loaded their wet, dripping catch into cardboard boxes in the back seats. This was before the days of plastic bags. The water had to have soaked into the seats. Anyone who has worked with fish knows that the odor is almost impossible to get out of fabric. I wonder if they ever got that fish smell out?

When the trout and salmon population began increasing during the late 1970s and '80s, the smelt decreased in number. As a result, people stopped coming to Lake Superior for smelting and we no longer needed to stay open all night to protect the property.

As the business grew, so did the building. Two more additions were built and we added more equipment; a deep fat fryer, a larger grill with two gas burners on the side, automatic coffee maker, deep freeze, another refrigerator and an automatic dish washer.

In the 1960s, we went smoke-free, becoming the first smoke-free restaurant in the state of Minnesota. Any smokers wishing to light up were invited to use "our outer lobby" at the picnic tables outside. This did not deter smokers from stopping for their pie and coffee. The restaurant was just too small and the food was too good to allow smoking in the same area.

More than pies were served in the restaurant. We had fresh trout, walleye, chicken and shrimp dinners. We had frozen fruit salad with a pineapple dressing and a whipped lime jello salad also served with the pineapple dressing. I served fresh homemade rye bread with all our meals, so there was a lot of baking besides the pies. We had hamburgers, hot dogs and sandwiches, all served on the homemade rye bread if the customer requested it. My day started at 4:30 a.m. and continued until 9 p.m. To ensure quality, I did all of the baking myself, including 24 loaves of bread a day, up to 100 pies, cookies, donuts and bars six days a week. This went on for six months. The other six months was my time to "play."

We chose Tuesdays as our day to be closed because it was the slowest day of the week and would affect the fewest number of customers. Originally I planned to use this day to catch up on my personal life, but I soon learned that I needed the day to shop for specific supplies I couldn't get from the food distributor. Tuesday also became valuable for a thorough, in-depth

cleaning. Gert Heil was my wonderful cleaning lady and I could always depend on her for quality work. She also gave me the recipe for lemon meringue pie that was a best-seller at the restaurant through the years.

The best fruit pies are made only with fresh fruits. This meant a very short season for some kinds of pie. Strawberries were available all summer long, but raspberries were available only for a month or so and blueberries and peaches for only about three to four weeks. Since our northern climate determined when the berries would be ripe, I always had a list of customers to call when the raspberries and blueberries came in. It's a very different world today, when fresh fruits are available year-round.

Knowledge of Betty's was passed by word of mouth. No advertising was done. In the 1980s, articles began appearing in area newspapers and Betty's now became known as "Betty's Pies." In 1983, Betty's was written up in the *Minneapolis Magazine*, *Duluth News-Tribune* and *St. Paul Pioneer Press* and

In the late 1960s, the dynamic force behind Betty's was Betty Lessard (left), husband Lloyd (center) and Betty's mom, Minnie Christiansen.

many out-of-state papers. Several customers reported reading about the wonderful pies at Betty's in the *Fargo Forum*. A number of customers came into the restaurant one Sunday saying, "We heard about this place from our minister's sermon." Looking for heavenly pies, no doubt.

Through all of this, business kept growing, especially the baking. It was now a busy six months of hard work, but each day was a challenge to see how much more I could do than I had done the day before, especially after Lloyd's death and my dad passing away in 1979.

June Heurlin, one of my customers, was a librarian from Chicago who fell in love with the north shore and wanted to move up here. She needed a place to live and in 1978 she ended up living with me and doing the prep work in the kitchen. Her company was especially good for me after losing Lloyd and my father in the 1970s. A couple of years later, the statistical record she compiled of my first 25 years in business astounded me.

This is what she wrote in 1981: "In 25 years, (her baking) adds up to 60,560 pies, or 423,920 pieces of pie. And that's not all. When it comes to donuts, she's made 389,700 of 'em and 175,500 cookies!! Wow! I can't forget the rye bread – every sandwich, except hamburgers and hot dogs, are made with Betty's rye and that adds up to 81,900 loaves! I'm pooped!!! Betty ought to be, but she's still on the job, turning out the goodies!"

That same year the scrapbooks show that our customers came from all 50 states, Washington, D.C., and 30 foreign countries.

All that hard work was always worthwhile when I'd see the smiling faces of happy customers. Through the years, waitresses have given me many notes written by customers that I really appreciated receiving, some of which are shared in this book.

I sold the restaurant in 1984 to enter retirement. The restaurant was resold in 1998 to Carl Ehlenz and Marti Sieber. Carl and Marti asked me to come back to advise and help them ensure that customers have the quality of pies they expect at Betty's. Since I really missed the customers, I gladly accepted their invitation. With the new Betty's Pies, it has been fun to walk in, give my advice, help out and then be able to walk out with no further responsibilities.

Since my retirement, I've found a new pleasure. In 1986, I got a standard schnauzer puppy named Tammy. She turned out to be a show dog,

In summer 2000, the new Betty's Pies opened behind the old building, increasing the space and modernizing the restaurant.

so off to California I went with her. She took top honors, then off to Canada and Washington, DC. After a couple of years with her, it was time to get another. Liesel is her name. Tammy is gone now, but I have Liesel and also Omega. I have given up training and showing them. Now I just enjoy having them. There is never a dull moment around this household and I love it that way.

Many thanks to all the wonderful customers who became such a part of my life. It was my pleasure to serve you for 28 years and to make so many wonderful acquaintances. I continue that friendship with many of you in my retirement.

I hope you enjoy these recipes as much as I enjoyed making them for you.

Betty Lessard, June 2001

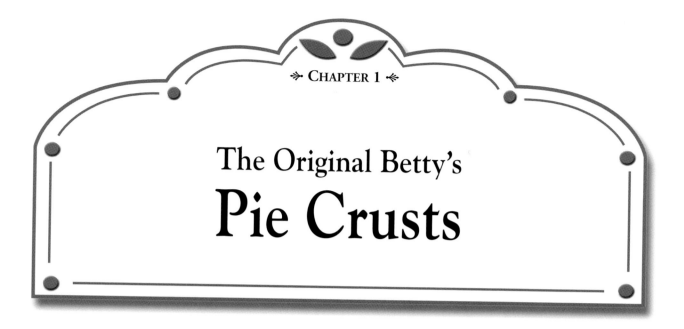

Chapter 1

The Original Betty's
Pie Crusts

For pastry crusts, I've always used Gold Medal-brand flour, because I know that flour and how much to use in my recipes. It's important to remember that each flour can be different from another. With some brands, you'll need to add more for a recipe, while others will require less flour.

In rolling out crusts, I use a pastry board that comes fitted with a cover and I also use a cover (cotton sock) on the rolling pin. This also works great when rolling out cookies, lefse and homemade noodles – I wouldn't be without mine. They can be purchased at a Swedish/Scandinavian shop and are a valuable addition to your baking utensils.

If you haven't yet added a food processor in your kitchen, they're a great appliance. They make it so easy to thoroughly mix dry ingredients and shortening for pastry crusts. You just dump the ingredients into the container and pulse the processor about 10 times until the shortening is about the size of a pea. Store this mixture in a covered bowl in the refrigerator until you're ready to roll out a crust, then add your liquid mixture just before you roll the crust.

PIE CRUSTS

Know Your Betty

After I sold my business, I began encountering former customers who recognized me on sight as Betty from Betty's Pies. This started when I took my first summer vacation in 28 years. We went to visit a friend in Billings on our way to Kalispell, Montana. This friend took us to lunch at one of the hotels in Billings. There were two young women sitting there and I didn't pay much attention to them. After we left Billings, we drove to Missoula and checked into a motel. I was out in the parking lot walking my dog, when these two gals came out of their room and called to me, "Hey, we want to talk to you." Now what, I thought. I don't know them, but I haven't done anything, so let them talk. They came over and one of them said, "We saw you at the hotel in Billings." I indicated that we had been there and she said, "You're Betty from Betty's Pies." I said yes. It ended up that they were nurses from Minneapolis and had been to the restaurant many times when they visited the north shore.

After the sale of Betty's Pies in 1984, Betty devoted more time to her animals, including her showdog Tammy (center) and Liesel (right). Betty prizes her rolling pin collection, which numbers in the hundreds. Whenever she rolls out pie crust, she uses a cotton "sock" around the pin.

Chocolate Wafer Crust

1 1/2 cups crumbs from chocolate wafer cookies*
1/4 cup sugar
1/4 cup butter or margarine, melted

Lightly butter the bottom and sides of a 9-inch pie pan. In a bowl combine the crumbs, sugar and melted butter. Press the mixture across the bottom and partway up the sides of the pan. Set aside. Fill with your desired filling.

*Chocolate wafer cookies, made by Nabisco and other companies, are different from Oreos and are sometimes difficult to find in groceries. Oreos can be used, however, if the frosting is removed from the chocolate cookie (see Oreo crust recipe page 17).

Graham Cracker Crust

2 cups graham cracker crumbs
1/2 cup powdered sugar
1/2 cup butter

In a bowl mix the graham cracker crumbs and powdered sugar. Melt the butter and add to the cracker crumbs and sugar. Mix until blended. Reserve 1/2 cup of the crumbs for the top.

Pat the balance of the crumbs in bottom and sides of the pie tin. Put in the refrigerator to set and get cold. Use as is with your favorite filling or bake, as with cheesecake.

Meringue Shell

4 large egg whites
1/4 teaspoon cream of tarter
1 cup granulated sugar

Preheat oven to 275°.

Beat egg whites until frothy. Add cream of tarter. Beat until stiff peaks form using electric mixer on high speed. Gradually add sugar, 2 Tablespoons at a time until one cup has been added. Continue beating until stiff, glossy peaks form.

Grease 10-inch pie pan and spread meringue on bottom and up sides of pie pan using a rubber scrapper.

Place on bottom rack in oven and bake at 275° for one hour. Turn off oven, open door ajar and let meringue cool in the oven. Fill with desired filling.

Comments

Recently, while applying for my new license tabs in Duluth, the woman behind the counter noticed that my plates read "Pielady" and asked if I was Betty from Betty's Pies. I told her that I was and the girl working with her asked, "You're Betty? Did you bring us a pie?" Most people don't even know my last name. They only know me as Betty, the pie baker.

By the early 1970s, Betty worked hard each day filling more than 100 pie pans.

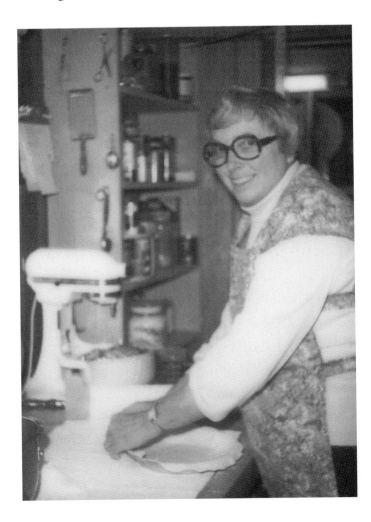

Nut Crust

1/4 cup packed brown sugar
1/2 cup butter
1 cup flour
1/2 cup chopped cashews

Mix the brown sugar, butter, flour and cashews together with a fork or pastry cutter. Spread in a cake pan and bake for 15 minutes at 325° or until lightly brown. Remove from oven and cool.

Crumble after it has cooled and press 3/4 of the crumbs on the bottom of a 10-inch pie pan.

Save 1/4 of the crumbs for the top of your pie.

I use butter in all of my recipes. In each case, unless specified, bring the butter to room temperature.

Oreo™ Cookie Crust

2 cups Oreo cookies, crushed
1/4 cup butter, melted

Put the cookies into a plastic bag and crush with a rolling pin. Put cookie crumbs into a small bowl and mix with melted butter.

Press into the bottom and sides of a 9-inch pie pan and place in the refrigerator for about 30 minutes then take out and fill with your favorite filling.

Pastry Crust Mix

5 1/2 cups flour, sifted
1 teaspoon salt
1 teaspoon baking powder
1 pound lard (I recommend Morrell-brand)

1 egg
1 cup milk, egg added

Milk is used for its liquid characteristics. In general throughout the book, unless noted, you can follow your preference and use whole, 2%, 1% or skim milk interchangeably.

I use Morrell lard because it is a firmer lard. I cut this into 1/2-inch to 1-inch cubes. Measure the flour into the food processor and add the salt and baking powder. Pulse a couple of times to mix this together. Add the cubes of lard and pulse about 10 times or until the lard pieces are about the size of a pea. Put this mixture into a bowl and cover. Store in the refrigerator until you want to roll out a pie shell.

Take out 3/4 cup of the mix to roll out one 9-inch pie shell (a bit more for a 10-inch shell). Put one egg into an ample measuring cup and add enough milk to make one cup liquid. Mix this so the egg gets blended.

Use 2 to 3 Tablespoons of this egg mixture as the liquid for the pie crust mix. If you get a little too much liquid, add a little mix so you can handle the dough. Roll this out using a pastry cloth and a cover on the rolling pin. Roll in every direction to about one inch larger than your pie tin. Fold it in half and slide it into your pie pan, unfolding across. Fold under the extra pie dough (if it is too much, cut extra off with a knife). Make a fluted edge with your fingers and prick the bottom and sides of the pie crust.

For unbaked pie recipes, bake the crust on the lower rack of the oven at 400° for about 10 minutes or until lightly brown. Remove from oven and cool.

CHAPTER 2

The Original Betty's
Baked Pies

I use flour mixed with sugar for my thickening when making baked pies. For very juicy pies like blueberry or bumble berry, it's a good idea to add a teaspoon of corn starch along with the flour to get added thickening. Peach, apple and blueberry have been favorites through all the years at Betty's Pies and bumble berry seems to be a year-round favorite. A friend from International Falls, Minnesota, would call ahead to tell me he was coming down to the north shore on such-and-such a day and wanted to pick up an apple pie. I'd be sure to have it waiting for him when he dropped in. My own favorite pie will always be fresh peach served warm with a scoop of ice cream – ummmm! (See Fresh Fruit Pies.)

BAKED PIES

The top pastry crust on all covered pies should be pierced several times with a fork to let steam escape during baking.

Lots and Lots of Baking

On a typical day, during the summer months, Betty and her helpers would start early in the morning preparing the pies and other goodies for the day's trade. First came the strawberry pies, the best seller. On Sundays, there were 100 pies to prepare.

"We'd stash pies anywhere they would fit, in the walk-in cooler, on shelves, counters, even boxes," Betty says. They would all be sold by early afternoon.

On a typical weekday, early in the year there would be 45 pies, which would increase to 60 or 65 per day at the height of the season. In addition to pies, the crew prepared 24 loaves of bread, donuts and cookies. Each day, all the products would sell out.

Apple Pie

7 tart apples (Granny Smiths are very good in pies)
1 cup packed brown sugar
2 Tablespoons granulated sugar
3 Tablespoons flour
1/2 teaspoon cinnamon

Peel and slice apples (about 1/4-inch thick). Mix brown sugar, granulated sugar, cinnamon and flour together. Mix with the apples. Roll out crust and place in a 10-inch pie pan. Pour in apples and dot with butter. Cover with top crust, pinch edges to seal, sprinkle with sugar, poke top crust a few times with a fork to let steam escape and bake in a 400° oven for 10 minutes. Reduce heat to 375° and bake about 40 to 45 minutes longer.

I recommend 10-inch pie tins for recipes that are likely to bubble over during baking, but you'll also save oven cleaning effort if you use a drip sheet under the pies.

Apple-Blueberry Pie

1 9-inch unbaked pie crust
4 cups peeled, sliced baking apples
2 cups fresh or frozen blueberries
3/4 cup packed brown sugar
1/4 cup granulated sugar
1/4 cup flour
1/2 teaspoon cinnamon
1 Tablespoon lemon juice

Topping
1 cup flour
1/2 cup packed brown sugar, firmly packed
1/4 teaspoon nutmeg
1/3 cup softened butter

This is my own creation. It started with my apple pie filling and I added blueberries, tried the pie on my tasters, made some adjustments in ingredients and it's been a favorite at the restaurant for years.

Preheat oven to 425°.

In large bowl, combine all filling ingredients and mix well – set aside.

For topping, lightly spoon flour into measuring cup, level off. In medium bowl, combine all topping ingredients, mix with fork until crumbly.

Spoon fruit into crust-lined pan. Sprinkle topping evenly over fruit.

Bake at 425° for 10 minutes, reduce heat to 375° and bake about 45 minutes or until apples are tender and edges are bubbly. Cover entire pie loosely with foil after 20 minutes to prevent excessive browning. Cool 2 hours. Serve warm or cold.

Fresh Cherry Pie

1 1/3 cups sugar
3 drops almond extract
1/3 cup flour
1/8 teaspoon salt
4 cups pitted tart fresh cherries
2 Tablespoons butter

Preheat oven to 400°.

Roll out a pie crust and line a 9-inch pie pan. Combine the sugar, flour, salt and mix well. Add the cherries and almond extract. Pour into the lined pie pan and dot with butter. Cover with a top crust, pinch edges to seal, pierce with a fork and sprinkle with sugar.

Bake in a 400° oven for 45 to 50 minutes.

GUEST CHECK

Comments

We had two couples come in from India. The women were dressed in their saris and the first thing they wanted to know was "what is pie?" They had been told to be sure to stop at Betty's for pie, but had no idea what pie was. We showed them our pies and explained to them the difference between cream pies, baked pies and fresh berry pies. They sat down and each ordered a different kind of pie. They passed them around so they could sample each one. Smiles on their faces and their remarks of "umm good" told us how well they liked our pie.

Pumpkin Pie

This is a light Pumpkin Pie that goes very well after a big Turkey Dinner. I got the recipe from my sister-in-law and it's the only one I ever used since then. The amount of liquid in the filling seems excessive, but you have to have it or the pie won't turn out well.

1 1/2 cups pumpkin
3/4 cup sugar (a little more)
1/2 teaspoon salt
1/2 teaspoon ginger
1 teaspoon cinnamon
1/4 teaspoon nutmeg
1/4 teaspoon cloves
4 eggs, slightly beaten
1 3/4 cups milk
3/4 cup evaporated milk

Preheat oven to 450°.

Whisk together pumpkin, sugar, salt and spices. Add beaten eggs, milk and evaporated milk. Pour into a 10-inch pie pan lined with an unbaked crust.

Bake at 450° for 10 minutes and reduce temp to 325° and bake for 50 minutes longer. Bake until a knife inserted in the center comes out clean. Cool and top with whipped cream.

Pecan Pie

1 9-inch unbaked pie crust
1 cup light corn syrup
1 cup dark brown sugar, firmly packed
3 eggs, slightly beaten
1/3 cup butter, melted
1/3 teaspoon salt
1 teaspoon vanilla extract
1 heaping cup pecans

Preheat oven to 350°.

Line pan with unbaked crust. In a large bowl, combine corn syrup, sugar, eggs, butter, salt and vanilla. Mix well. Pour filling into prepared pie crust; sprinkle with pecan halves.

Bake for 45 to 50 minutes or until center is set. Toothpick inserted will come out clean when pie is done. Cool.

Comments

I had a special final customer every year. During our season, he'd ride his bicycle up from Duluth fairly often and stop for pie. On the last day of each season he'd order seven different kinds of pie and tell me, "Just put them down on the counter in front of me." He would start with the one on his left and work his way right down the line until he had eaten all seven pieces! "Now, that'll hold me 'til you open next year," he always said as he left.

The Original Betty's
Baked Fresh Fruit Pies

FRESH FRUIT PIES

I can't even guess how many crates of fresh strawberries I've used through the years, but many longtime customers will remember Mother and Dad sitting at the back table in the old Betty's cleaning 10 crates of strawberries every Saturday for me to use on Sunday. Another favorite was the fresh fruit pie I made with strawberries, raspberries and blueberries. My good friend Chuck Elving, who lives about 10 miles up the road from me, always kept me supplied with fresh raspberries when they were in season. He had a great berry patch and soon found out that if I didn't get them, the bears would. He picked them in the late afternoon and brought them down so I could have pies first thing in the morning.

A Berry Wild Pie

One day in August at about closing time, four couples arrived on their motorcycles. They were from a church in Iowa and were going to have supper and were all set to order fresh blueberry pie for dessert. I told them that I was all out of fresh blueberry pie. They were so disappointed that I said if they could all agree on what kind of pie they wanted, I would make it for them while they ate their supper. They all agreed on blueberry cream, which I made and served to them. They also wanted to pick wild blueberries, so I told them about a spot near Palisade Head, where I knew there was good berry picking. They asked if they picked the blueberries and brought them in to me the next morning, would I make a pie for them. I said yes. The next morning about 10 a.m., they walked in with a bucket of blueberries. I told them to come back in a couple of hours and I'd have their pie ready. They said, "We had our special pie last night. These berries are to thank you." They left the blueberries and went on their way. They were a great group and we became good friends. We still keep in touch.

The top pastry crust on all covered pies should be pierced several times with a fork to let steam escape during baking. For pies with a top crust, see the procedure for Cherry Pie on page 31.

June Heurlin was my "right-hand man" for 20 years. Originally from Chicago, she showed up one day looking for a new way of life. She was one of the people who encouraged me to complete this book. She passed away late in 2000.

Baked Blueberry Pie

1 cup sugar
5 Tablespoons flour
1/4 teaspoon cinnamon
4 cups fresh or frozen blueberries
1 1/3 Tablespoons butter

Preheat oven to 400°.

Make pastry for two-crust pie. Line a 9-inch pie pan with a rolled-out pie crust. Combine the sugar, flour and cinnamon and mix well. Mix lightly with 4 cups blueberries and pour into pastry-lined pie pan. Dot with the butter and cover with a top crust, pierce with a fork and sprinkle with sugar.

Bake for 20 minutes in a 400° oven, then turn oven down to 375° and bake additional 30 to 35 minutes.

Of all the pies I made through the years, fresh wild blueberry and fresh peach pie are the only ones that I would die for.

Bumble Berry Pie

1 cup blueberries
1 cup blackberries
1 cup strawberries
1 cup raspberries
1 cup sugar
5 Tablespoons flour
2 Tablespoons corn starch
1/2 teaspoon cinnamon

Preheat oven to 375°.

Line a 10-inch pie pan with crust.

Combine the sugar, flour, corn starch and cinnamon and mix well. Lightly mix in the fresh fruit and pour into the pie shell.

Dot with butter and cover with a top crust. Prick the crust and sprinkle with sugar.

Bake at 375° for 35 minutes in a convection oven* or 50 minutes in a regular oven.

This has become a real favorite at the restaurant since new owners Carl Ehlenz and Marti Sieber took over.

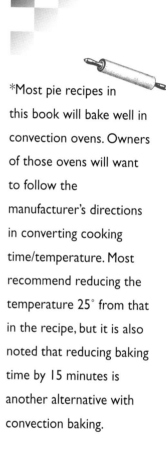

*Most pie recipes in this book will bake well in convection ovens. Owners of those ovens will want to follow the manufacturer's directions in converting cooking time/temperature. Most recommend reducing the temperature 25° from that in the recipe, but it is also noted that reducing baking time by 15 minutes is another alternative with convection baking.

Cherry Berry Pie

2 cups pitted tart fresh or frozen cherries
1 cup fresh or frozen raspberries
1 cup fresh or frozen blueberries
1 cup sugar
2 Tablespoons corn starch
2 Tablespoons flour
1 teaspoon cinnamon
butter

Preheat oven to 400°.

Combine the sugar, corn starch, flour and cinnamon. Toss the berries lightly and put into unbaked pie shell. Dot with butter and cover with top crust. Prick the crust and sprinkle with sugar.

Bake at 400° for 15 minutes, then reduce heat to 375° and bake for about 40 minutes.

Cherry Pie

2 14.5- to 16-oz. cans tart red cherries in water, drained
1 1/4 cups sugar
2 1/2 Tablespoons flour
1/4 teaspoon salt
butter

Preheat oven to 450°.

Divide pastry almost in half. Roll out the larger half on a floured surface to a 13-inch circle. Line 9-inch pie plate with pastry. Trim edge to 1 inch beyond rim of pie plate.

Combine cherries, sugar, flour and salt in a bowl; mix well. Spoon cherry mixture into pastry-lined pie plate. Dot with butter.

Roll out the other half of the pastry and cover the cherry mixture. Press and seal edges. Prick the crust with a fork and sprinkle with sugar.

Bake at 450° for 10 minutes. Reduce temperature to 350° and bake 30 minutes more or until crust is golden brown. Cool on rack.

Because fresh cherries were available such a short time years ago, this became a staple at Betty's during the "non-cherry" season, which was most of the time we were open. It was a very steady and good seller throughout the years. Today, with cherries available much longer during the year, fresh cherry pie can be offered to customers much of the season.

Cranberry-Apple Pie with Crunch Topping

1 lightly baked pie crust
1/4 cup gingersnap cookie crumbs

4 medium tart green apples, sliced thin
    (Granny Smiths work well)
1 1/2 cups frozen or fresh cranberries
1/2 cup raisins
1 cup sugar
2 Tablespoons flour
1 Tablespoon corn starch
2 teaspoons grated lemon peel
1/4 teaspoon nutmeg

Topping
3/4 cup old-fashioned oatmeal
1/2 cup chopped pecans
1/3 cup packed brown sugar
6 Tablespoons butter
1/3 cup flour
1/2 teaspoon cinnamon

Preheat oven to 375°.

Combine apples, cranberries and raisins in bowl. Add sugar, 2 Tablespoons flour, corn starch, lemon peel, 1/4 teaspoon nutmeg. Toss to coat fruit. Put in shell and press to compact.

Topping: Mix oatmeal, pecans, brown sugar, butter, remaining 1/3 cup flour and cinnamon. Mix until moist clumps form and sprinkle over filling. Cover filling completely.

Bake at 375° for about 40 to 45 minutes.

Fresh Peach Pie
(Betty's Favorite)

1 cup sugar
5 Tablespoons flour
1/2 teaspoon cinnamon
4 1/2 cups sliced peaches
1 1/2 Tablespoons butter

Preheat oven to 400°.

Line a 9-inch pie pan with pastry.

Combine the 1 cup of sugar, flour and cinnamon, mixing well. Lightly mix in the fresh peaches and pour into the pie shell. Dot with butter and cover with a top crust. Prick the top crust and sprinkle with sugar.

Put the pie into a 400° oven and bake for 40 to 50 minutes.

Peach is my favorite of all the pies. Even today when I bake this pie, I think of one of the girls who worked for me, because she was the first one to have a piece of warm peach pie. She lived up the road from the restaurant and would always walk down for pie when she knew I was baking it.

Rhubarb Pie

4 cups cut-up rhubarb
1 1/2 cups sugar
6 Tablespoons flour
1 1/3 Tablespoons butter

Preheat oven to 425°.

Mix sugar and flour together. Add cut-up rhubarb. Roll out pie crust and place in a 10-inch pie pan. Pour rhubarb mixed with sugar and flour into pie pan. Dot with butter and cover with top crust, prick to let steam escape and sprinkle with sugar. Bake in a 425° oven for 40 to 50 minutes.

I always add one Tablespoon of strawberry-flavored gelatin powder to the flour and sugar mixture to give a nice bright color to the pie. If you do this, cut the flour mixture to 5 Tablespoons.

Rhubarb-Strawberry Cream Pie

1 unbaked pie shell
3 eggs, separated
1/2 cup sweet cream
1/2 teaspoon salt
1 1/4 cups sugar
2 Tablespoons all-purpose flour
3 cups diced rhubarb
6 large strawberries sliced or
    1/2 10-oz. package frozen strawberries in syrup
6 Tablespoons sugar

Preheat oven to 400°.

Beat egg yolks. Add cream and beat again. Mix salt, sugar and flour together and add to the egg mixture. Put diced rhubarb in unbaked pie shell; pour egg mixture over it. Add strawberries.

Bake at 400° for 10 minutes, reduce heat to 350° and bake for another 30 minutes.

Beat egg whites until stiff; add 6 Tablespoons sugar. Spread meringue on pie to cover and bake for an additional 30 minutes at 300°.

Strawberry-Rhubarb Pie

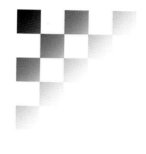

1 1/4 cups sugar
1/3 cup flour
1/8 teaspoon salt
1 pint fresh strawberries, cleaned & hulled
2 cups cut-up rhubarb
2 Tablespoons butter

Preheat oven to 400°.

Make enough pastry for a 2-crust pie. Roll out one-half of pastry on a floured surface to a 13-inch circle. Line a 9-inch pie plate with the pastry.

Mix together 1 1/4 cups sugar, flour and salt in a bowl. Combine strawberries and rhubarb in another bowl, mix well. Arrange half of the fruit mixture in the bottom of the pastry-lined pie plate. Sprinkle with half of the sugar mixture. Repeat with remaining fruit and sugar mixture. Dot with butter.

Roll out other half of pastry to a 11-inch circle. Place top crust over filling and trim edges to 1-inch beyond the rim of the pie plate. Fold top crust under lower crust and form a ridge. Flute edge. Pierce with fork and sprinkle with sugar.

Bake for 20 minutes at 400°, lower temperature to 375° and continue baking for 30 to 35 minutes. Cool on rack.

The Original Betty's
Special Pies

Continued

The Lemon Angel, Chocolate Layer, Mint Chocolate and Orange Chocolate pies are great because they can be made ahead and keep nicely in the refrigerator for a few days. They also freeze well. I always have Chocolate Layer Pie, cut into serving size pieces, in my freezer to serve if someone drops in unexpectedly or I have guests arrive on short notice. If you freeze the Lemon Angel Pie, I think it's actually better if served while still slightly frozen.

Some people like to melt their chocolate in the microwave, but I've always preferred using a saucepan, constantly stirring. If you are worried about burning, put the saucepan into another pan of boiling water, creating a double boiler.

All Good Scouts

My normal summer day began at 5 a.m. with setting the bread to rise, then starting the pies so I'd be ready to open the restaurant at 11 a.m. One morning, a troop of Boy Scouts pulled in at about 9:30 a.m. and the scoutmaster came to the back window where I was working. He told me that one of the boys was having a birthday and his parents had given him money so they could stop at Betty's and have pie. A bit reluctantly I said, "Well, okay, I'll open the door and let you in."

The only one there to help was June, my friend from Chicago who had become enthralled with the North Shore, moved up here and stayed at my home. I had her doing all my prep work and she was working in the back room. She became an instant waitress – which was definitely not her calling.

We seated all the boys and started serving them. Then, of course I couldn't lock the door, because other customers immediately began to come in, assuming that we were open for the day. When the waitresses began arriving at about 10:30 or 10:45, we had a pretty big crowd and they questioned if they were late for work or what was going on. As soon as they walked in the back door, June said, "Here! You can have your job. I'm not a waitress. I don't want the job."

They took over. That day we opened at 9:30 a.m., which made a long day, but that group of Boy Scouts was very happy! Years later, I had some of them return with families of their own and thank me for my kindness. They never forgot that day.

Chocolate Peanut Pie

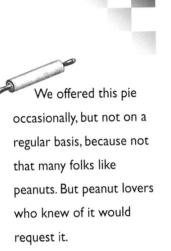

We offered this pie occasionally, but not on a regular basis, because not that many folks like peanuts. But peanut lovers who knew of it would request it.

1 9-inch unbaked pie crust
2/3 cup semisweet chocolate chips
3 eggs
1 cup light corn syrup
1/3 cup sugar
2 Tablespoons butter, melted
1 teaspoon vanilla extract
1 1/2 cups roasted salted peanuts
Whipped cream for garnish

Preheat the oven to 350°.

Fit the pie crust into a 9-inch pan. Put the pie pan on a baking sheet. Melt the chocolate in a small saucepan over very low heat, stirring frequently to avoid burning. Cool slightly. Meanwhile, beat the eggs in a large bowl until they are frothy. Add the corn syrup, sugar, melted butter, vanilla and the cooled chocolate and beat well. Stir in the peanuts. Pour into prepared shell and bake at 350° about 50 to 60 minutes, until a knife inserted in the center comes out clean. Cool on a rack. Serve warm or at room temperature topped with whipped cream.

Chocolate Layer Pie
(Also called Five Layer Chocolate)

1 9-inch baked pie shell

Meringue
2 egg whites
1/2 teaspoon white vinegar
1/2 cup sugar
1/4 teaspoon salt
1/4 teaspoon cinnamon

2 egg yolks slightly beaten
1/4 cup cold water
1 cup semi-sweet chocolate chips

1 cup heavy cream, whipped
1/4 cup sugar
1/4 teaspoon cinnamon

Preheat the oven to 325°.

Beat egg whites until frothy, add vinegar, beating until soft mounds form. Gradually add the 1/2 cup sugar with 1/4 teaspoon salt and 1/4 teaspoon cinnamon and beat until meringue stands in stiff glossy peaks. Spread on bottom and sides of the baked pie shell. Bake at 325° for 20 minutes or until lightly browned. Cool.

Combine the egg yolks, water and semi-sweet chocolate chips and melt over a very low heat until chips are melted. Spread 3 Tablespoons of this over the cooled meringue. Cool.

Whip the cream until thick and add the sugar and cinnamon. Spread half of this over the chocolate layer.

Combine remaining whipped cream with the remaining chocolate mixture. Spread this over the whipped cream in the pie shell. Cool at least 4 hours.

This, Fresh Strawberry and Lemon Angel pies were the three best-sellers during the time I operated Betty's Pies. People would line up in our little parking lot on weekends to get these pies.

Dreamy High Pumpkin Pie

This is also a nice light pumpkin pie, like the baked pumpkin pie (page 24) that I recommended serving after a big holiday meal.

1 10-inch baked pie shell or graham cracker crust
2/3 cup sugar
1 envelope unflavored gelatin
1 teaspoon ground cinnamon
1/2 teaspoon salt
1/4 teaspoon nutmeg
3 slightly beaten egg yolks
3/4 cup milk
1 cup canned pumpkin
3 egg whites
1/3 cup sugar
1/2 cup heavy cream, whipped
1/2 cup flaked coconut, toasted

In a large sauce pan, combine the 2/3 cup sugar, the unflavored gelatin, cinnamon, salt and nutmeg. Combine beaten egg yolks and milk; add to gelatin mixture. Cook, stirring constantly, until mixture thickens slightly. Stir in pumpkin. Chill until mixture mounds slightly when spooned (about 10 minutes), stirring often.

Beat egg whites until soft peaks form. Gradually add the 1/3 cup sugar, beating to stiff peaks. Fold chilled pumpkin mixture into egg whites. Pile into prepared crust. Chill until firm, about 2 hours.

Just before serving, whip cream and spoon on top of pie. Sprinkle with toasted coconut.

French Silk Pie

1 9-inch baked pie shell
1/2 pound butter
2 cups powdered sugar
2 Tablespoons vanilla extract
2 squares (1 oz.) unsweetened baking chocolate
4 extra large eggs

Whip the powdered sugar, butter and vanilla together for 5 minutes. Melt 2 squares of bitter chocolate and add to the sugar, butter mixture and beat for 5 minutes. Add 4 eggs, 1 at a time; beat for 5 minutes after each addition. After adding the last egg, beat for 8 minutes. Pour into a baked pie shell and refrigerate. Top with whipped cream.

This has always been a big seller at the restaurant.

I'M NOT BETTY

Note: nutritionists recommend that foods using uncooked egg ingredients be kept hot, cold or be used or disposed of within four hours of preparation.

Frozen Peanut Butter Pie

1 chocolate pie crust (purchased)
1 1/2 cups powdered sugar
1 cup peanut butter (smooth or crunchy)
1 8-oz. package cream cheese, softened
1/2 teaspoon vanilla extract
1 cup heavy cream, whipped

Blend sugar, peanut butter, cream cheese and vanilla until smooth. Transfer to a large bowl. In a separate bowl, beat whipping cream to form soft peaks. Fold half the peanut butter mixture into the cream – then fold in the other half. Pour into pie shell and freeze 3 hours or more. Let stand at room temperature 20 minutes before serving.

Hershey Bar™ Pie

15 marshmallows
1/2 cup milk
3/4 cup (about 5 small 1.5 oz.) Hershey bars, melted
1/2 pint heavy cream, whipped

Melt the marshmallows and 1/2 cup of milk in double boiler and add melted Hershey bars. Let cool. Whip 1/2 pint of cream until stiff and fold in cooled mixture.

Crust
1/3 cup powdered sugar
1/2 cup butter
18 graham crackers, crushed

Mix thoroughly; reserve 1/2 cup for top of pie. With the rest, pat into pie tin and fill with the marshmallow mixture. Put balance of crumbs on top. Refrigerate several hours.

This recipe came from my cousin in California. Both the Frozen Peanut Butter and this one keep wonderfully in a freezer/refrigerator for those times when folks drop in unexpectedly and you want to serve a nice treat with coffee.

Lemon Angel Pie

Meringue Crust
4 egg whites
1 cup sugar
1/4 teaspoon cream of tartar

Filling
4 egg yolks
1/2 cup sugar
3 Tablespoons lemon juice

1 cup heavy cream, whipped

Beat the 4 egg whites well. Add cream of tarter. Gradually add sugar, 2 Tablespoons at a time until one cup has been added. Spread into bottom and up the sides of a greased 9-inch pie pan and bake at 275° for 1 hour. Cool.

Beat the 4 egg yolks and stir in 1/2 cup sugar, 3 Tablespoons lemon juice. Cook over low heat until thick. Cool.

Whip 1 cup cream and add to the above custard. Pour into the meringue shell and chill at least 2 hours.

Lemon Angel Pie is the name that Betty's Pies uses. It's a wonderful recipe that some recipe books call "On a Cloud Pie." The lemon-flavored pie just melts in your mouth.

Lemon Meringue Pie

Gert Heil, my wonderful cleaning lady, gave me this recipe years ago. It's an old standard and a favorite that I made sure to have at all times.

1 9-inch baked pie shell
1 1/2 cups sugar
5 1/3 Tablespoons corn starch
1 1/2 cups boiling water
4 egg yolks, lightly beaten
3 Tablespoons butter
4 Tablespoons lemon juice
1 1/3 Tablespoons grated lemon rind

Special Meringue Additive
2 Tablespoons sugar
1 Tablespoon corn starch
1/2 cup cold water

Meringue
4 egg whites
1/4 teaspoon cream of tartar
8 Tablespoons sugar

Preheat the oven to 400°.

Combine the sugar and corn starch and add to the boiling water. Cook over medium heat until thick. Slowly add *a little* of this hot mixture into the 4 lightly beaten egg yolks and stir. Combine both mixtures and cook 1 minute longer. Remove from heat and add the butter, lemon juice and grated rind. Pour into a baked pie shell and cover with the meringue.

Special Meringue Additive: To keep meringue from weeping, combine 2 Tablespoons sugar, 1 Tablespoon corn starch and 1/2 cup cold water. Mix and boil until thick and clear, then cool while whipping egg whites for meringue.

Meringue: Beat 4 egg whites with 1/4 teaspoon cream of tartar. Add the cooled cooked special additive. Continue beating; slowly add 8 Tablespoons of sugar. Cover top of lemon filling, making sure to seal edges of pie. Place in a 400° oven for 15 to 20 minutes. Remove and cool on wire rack.

Key Lime Pie

1/2 cup key lime juice
1 can sweetened condensed milk
1 8-oz. container Cool Whip™

Put the sweetened condensed milk into a bowl and slowly add the key-lime juice. Mix until creamy.

When creamy add the container of Cool Whip. Put into a graham cracker crust and refrigerate. If desired, garnish with additional Cool Whip and chocolate curls.

This is one pie that is quite regional in character and there are almost as many recipes for Key Lime Pie as we'd have customers asking for it at the restaurant. This one is my own favorite.

These days, Betty's family consists of her schnauzers, Falcon (left), Liesel (center) and Omega (next to Betty).

Macadamia Nut Chiffon Pie

4 egg yolks
1/2 cup granulated sugar
1/2 teaspoon salt
1 cup milk
1 envelope unflavored gelatin
1/4 cup cold water
4 egg whites
dash of salt
1/2 cup sugar
1/4 teaspoon almond extract
1 cup heavy cream, whipped
1/4 cup chopped macadamia nuts

In a small saucepan combine egg yolks, 1/2 cup sugar, 1/2 teaspoon salt and milk. Cook and stir until thickened. (Do not boil). Remove from heat and add gelatin, which has been dissolved in 1/4 cup cold water. Cool. Beat egg whites until soft peaks form and gradually add 1/2 cup sugar, beating until stiff. Fold into yolk mixture with almond extract. Pour into baked pie shell and top with whipped cream. Sprinkle top with 1/4 cup chopped macadamia nuts.

Mile High Pie

Pie Crust
1/4 cup packed brown sugar
1/2 cup butter, softened
1 cup flour
1/2 cup chopped cashews

Filling
1 10-oz. package frozen strawberries, thawed
2 egg whites
1 cup sugar
2 teaspoons lemon juice

1 cup heavy cream, whipped

This pie is great to have in the freezer for those unexpected visitors. It looks great and keeps very well.

Preheat oven to 350°.

Mix the brown sugar, butter, flour and nuts together, put in a pan and bake for 15 minutes at 350°. Crumble after it has cooled and press 3/4 of the crumbs on the bottom of a 10-inch pie pan.

Filling: Whip the strawberries, egg whites, sugar and lemon juice for 20 minutes with electric beater on high. Whip the cream and add to the strawberry mixture and pour over crumbs in pie pan. Top with remaining crumbs and store in the freezer.

Before serving, put in the refrigerator for about two hours.

Mint Chocolate Layer Pie

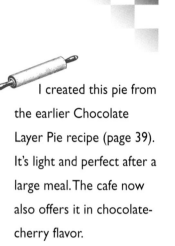

I created this pie from the earlier Chocolate Layer Pie recipe (page 39). It's light and perfect after a large meal. The cafe now also offers it in chocolate-cherry flavor.

1 9-inch baked pie shell

Meringue
2 egg whites
1/2 teaspoon white vinegar
1/4 teaspoon salt
1/2 cup sugar

Filling
2 egg yolks slightly beaten
1/4 cup cold water
1/2 cup mint chips
1/2 cup semi-sweet chocolate chips

Topping
1 cup heavy cream, whipped
1/4 cup sugar

Preheat the oven to 325°.

Meringue: Beat egg whites till frothy, add vinegar and salt, beating until soft mounds form. Gradually add the half cup sugar and beat until meringue stands in stiff glossy peaks. Spread on bottom and sides of the baked pie shell. Bake at 325° for 18 to 20 minutes or until lightly browned. Cool.

In a saucepan, combine the egg yolks, water, mint chips and semi-sweet chips and stir constantly over very low heat until chips are melted. Spread 3 Tablespoons of this over the cooled meringue. Chill remainder.

Whip the cream until thick and add the sugar. Spread half of this over the chocolate layer.

Combine remaining whipped cream with the chocolate mixture. Spread this over the whipped cream in the pie shell. Chill at least 4 hours.

Orange Chocolate Pie

Meringue
4 egg whites
1/4 teaspoon cream of tartar
1 cup sugar

Filling
1/2 cup sugar
1/2 teaspoon salt
4 egg yolks, beaten
2 Tablespoons orange juice
1 Tablespoon lemon juice
1 cup heavy cream, whipped
2 1.5-oz. milk chocolate bars, grated

Preheat the oven to 275°.

Meringue: Whip egg whites until foamy, add cream of tartar and continue beating with electric mixer at high speed. Gradually add the sugar, beating until stiff. Spread meringue in bottom and sides of a well-buttered 9-inch pie pan. Bake at 275° for 1 hour. Open the oven door and turn off the heat. Let the meringue cool in the oven.

Filling: While the meringue is baking, cook the filling and set aside to cool. Combine sugar, salt, beaten egg yolks, orange juice and lemon juice in a small saucepan. Cook over low heat stirring constantly until the mixture thickens. Remove from heat. Cool completely. Whip cream until stiff peaks form. Set aside. Take 1 1.5-oz. grated chocolate bar and spread into the cooled meringue shell. Combine the whipped cream and the cooled filling. Gently put into the meringue shell over the grated chocolate. Spread and cover the filling with the other grated chocolate bar. Cover and refrigerate 8 hours or overnight.

This is a wonderful recipe, but I had to make a few modifications to get it to work. The restaurant is still serving it, but be sure to follow the directions exactly to avoid disappointment.

Oreo™ Ice Cream Pie

Oreo Crust
25 Oreo cookies, crushed
1/2 cup butter, melted

Oreo Fudge Topping
1/3 cup butter
1 1/2 cups powdered sugar
1 cup evaporated milk
1/2 cup chocolate chips
1 teaspoon vanilla extract
1/2 gallon vanilla ice cream
1 1/2 cup Spanish peanuts, crushed slightly

Crush Oreo cookies and mix with melted butter. Line large pie pan with the Oreo crust. 11-inch pie plate or 2 smaller ones will do. Place in refrigerator until ready to use.

Mix 1/3 cup butter, evaporated milk, chocolate chips and powdered sugar in a sauce pan. Boil for 8 minutes, stirring constantly. Add vanilla and cool. Soften ice cream. Spoon softened vanilla ice cream over crust.

1st layer: crushed Oreos

2nd layer: softened vanilla ice cream

3rd layer: Spanish peanuts

4th layer: cooled fudge sauce

If desired, you can put a layer of caramel sauce on the top. Store in freezer until ready to serve.

Peanut Butter Pie

1 9-inch baked pie shell
4 oz. cream cheese
1 1/2 cups powdered sugar
1/2 cup chunky peanut butter
1/2 cup milk
1 1/2 cups heavy cream, whipped

With an electric mixer, beat the cream cheese, powdered sugar, peanut butter and milk and mix until creamy. Whip the cream and fold into the creamed mixture. Sprinkle chopped nuts on the top of the pie. Keep in the refrigerator until serving time.

This was a favorite of a doctor from the Twin Cities who spent time on the North Shore. I always tried to have it when she was coming up. She was killed in 2000 on a medical mission in Cameroon.

Betty displays some of the "samples" offered at the restaurant in the 1980s.

Raisin Buttermilk Pie

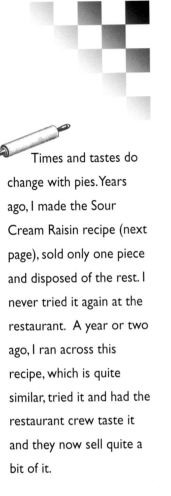

Times and tastes do change with pies. Years ago, I made the Sour Cream Raisin recipe (next page), sold only one piece and disposed of the rest. I never tried it again at the restaurant. A year or two ago, I ran across this recipe, which is quite similar, tried it and had the restaurant crew taste it and they now sell quite a bit of it.

1 9-inch baked pie shell
1 1/2 cups sugar
6 Tablespoons corn starch
1/4 teaspoon salt
3 egg yolks
3 cups buttermilk
3/4 cup raisins
3 Tablespoons lemon juice
1 Tablespoon butter
1 teaspoon vanilla extract

Meringue
3 egg whites
1/4 teaspoon cream of tartar
6 Tablespoons sugar

In a saucepan, combine sugar, corn starch and salt. Beat egg yolks and buttermilk; stir into the sugar mixture until smooth. Add raisins and lemon juice; cook and stir over medium heat until mixture comes to a gentle boil. Cook and stir 2 minutes longer. Remove from the heat; stir in butter and vanilla. Pour into pie shell.

Meringue: Beat egg whites and cream of tartar in a mixing bowl until soft peaks form. Gradually add sugar, beating until stiff peaks form. Spread over hot filling and seal to the edges of the pie curst. Bake at 350° for 12 to 15 minutes or until lightly browned. Store in the refrigerator.

Raisin Sour Cream Pie

1 9-inch baked pie shell
1/2 cup sugar
1/2 cup sour cream
2 Tablespoons corn starch
1/2 teaspoon salt
1/2 teaspoon cinnamon
2 egg yolks
3/4 cup milk
1 cup raisins

Meringue
2 egg whites
1/2 cup sugar

Preheat oven to 375°.

Mix the sugar, cream, corn starch, salt and cinnamon together.

Separate the eggs. Mix the egg yolks with the milk and add to the sugar mixture. Bring to a boil.

Stir in the raisins and cool. Put mixture in pie shell.

Meringue: While pie is cooling, beat the 2 egg whites until they are stiff. Gradually add 1/2 cup sugar and whip until they are glossy. Top the pie with this meringue and bake for 15 minutes at 375°.

A man came in and sat down at the counter. I went over, greeted him and talked to him for a minute or two. When he was ready to leave, he said, "I'll never forget you or this place."

"Why?" I asked.

"Because when I come in, you always greet me with a smile and that means a lot." And it's true. If someone came in tired after traveling, it was always a challenge to me to make them smile, relax and be friendly. I'm happy to say that most of the time I succeeded.

Raspberry or Strawberry Pie

When you operate a restaurant, you sometimes have to go well out of your way to please the customer. One day, a man came in who was on a special diet. He couldn't eat anything that was on our menu, but asked if I would make him a bowl of oatmeal? I cooked and served his oatmeal and was happy to do so. It meant a lot to him and I'm sure he told others about us – which is the best advertising possible. I always took pleasure in doing special favors for customers.

1 9-inch baked pie shell
3/4 cup water
4 cups raspberries or strawberries, washed and drained
3 Tablespoons corn starch
1 cup sugar
1 teaspoon lemon juice
1 cup heavy cream, whipped

Line baked, cooled pie shell with 3 cups of berries, reserving 1 cup for glaze. Simmer the 1 cup of berries and the water in sauce pan 3 to 4 minutes; strain the juice. Combine corn starch and sugar. Cook the juice with the corn starch and sugar until syrup is thick and clear, stirring constantly. Add lemon juice. Cool slightly. Pour over berries in pie shell. Chill thoroughly. Top with sweetened whipped cream.

Rhubarb Fluff Pie

1 graham cracker crust
4 cups rhubarb, diced
2 cups sugar
1 3-oz. package strawberry gelatin
20 large marshmallows
1/2 pint whipping cream

Cook the rhubarb and sugar together until soft. Do NOT add water. Stir in the gelatin until dissolved. Add marshmallows and mix. Let this cool, stirring occasionally. When cooled, whip cream and fold it into the cooked mixture. Pour into a graham cracker crust (see page 15). Refrigerate.

Snow Pie with Raspberry Sauce

1 9-inch baked pie shell
1 cup water
1/2 cup sugar
Pinch of salt
2 1/2 Tablespoons corn starch
3 egg whites
1 teaspoon vanilla extract
1 cup whipping cream

Boil water, sugar and salt, stirring until clear. Mix the corn starch with 1 Tablespoon cold water and add to the cooked mixture. Stir and cook until clear and bubbly. Set aside while beating egg whites. Add vanilla to whites. Pour the cooled mixture over the stiffly beaten egg whites and fold in well. Pile into a baked shell. Top with whipped cream when ready to serve.

Raspberry Sauce for Snow Pie
1/3 cup sugar
2 Tablespoons corn starch
1/2 cup water
1 10-oz. package frozen raspberries
Few drops of lemon juice

Stir together sugar and corn starch in small saucepan. Stir in water and raspberries. Cook and stir until mixture thickens and comes to a boil. Add the lemon juice and cool. Refrigerate. Drizzle over each piece of snow pie at serving time.

Toasted Coconut Lemon Pie

Meringue Crust
4 egg whites
1 teaspoon cream of tartar
1 cup sugar

Preheat oven to 250°.

Beat egg whites and cream of tartar until stiff. Gradually add 1 cup of sugar and beat well. Spread the meringue on the bottom and sides of a well-greased 9- or 10-inch pie pan. Bake for 1 hour at 250°. Remove from oven and cool.

Filling
4 egg yolks
1/2 cup sugar
Juice and rind of 1 1/2 lemons
1/2 pint whipping cream
Toasted coconut

Beat 4 egg yolks and add 1/2 cup sugar and juice and rind of 1 1/2 lemons. Cook on low heat until thick. Set aside to cool. When the meringue crust is cool, spread the lemon filling into the meringue shell. Whip 1/2 pint of cream and spread on top of the lemon filling. Sprinkle with toasted coconut and refrigerate overnight. Keep in the refrigerator.

Toffee Pie

1 9-inch baked pie crust
1 3.4-oz. package vanilla instant pudding & pie filling
1 1/4 cups milk
dash of salt
1 cup chopped Heath™ candy bars or toffee bits
2 cups whipped cream or Cool Whip™

Combine pudding mix with milk; whisk until thoroughly blended. Add salt and candy. Fold in whipped cream and pour into baked pie crust. Refrigerate.

This is really rich, but really good. A little goes a long way.

CHAPTER 5

The Original Betty's
Cream Pies

CREAM PIES

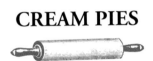

Banana Cream and Coconut Cream pies will always be big sellers and are favorites in home kitchens. Also, by adding a few cut-up strawberries and a little strawberry glazing to the Banana Cream recipe, you have an entirely new variety of pie that you can whip up on short notice.

All the cream pies are relatively easy and quick to make – but yummy. Many of my customers became quite devoted to their own favorites through the years, and if I knew they were coming, I'd make sure to have their choice of pie on hand for them.

Not Just for Angels

The Lemon Angel Pie (page 43), one of Betty's favorites, is one of the top sellers at Betty's Pies. The order of popularity: Strawberry, Chocolate Layer, Lemon Angel and Banana Cream.

Banana Cream Pie

1 9-inch baked pie shell or graham cracker shell
1 3.4-oz. package banana instant pudding & pie filling
1 1/4 cups milk
1 pint whipping cream
2 large bananas sliced

Mix the pudding mix and milk together until stiff. Store in refrigerator while whipping cream. Save about half of the whipped cream for the top of the pie. Fold the pudding mix into the other half of whipped cream. Slice bananas on top of a 9-inch pie shell. Cover the bananas with the pudding mix and top with the remaining whipped cream.

Coconut Cream Pie

1 9-inch baked pie shell or graham cracker shell
1 3.4-oz. package coconut cream instant pudding
   & pie filling
1 1/4 cups milk
1 pint whipping cream
1 1/2 cups coconut
Toasted coconut for top of pie

Mix the pudding mix and milk together until stiff. Store in refrigerator while whipping cream. Save about half the cream for the top of the pie. Fold the pudding mix into the whipped cream and fold in the 1 1/2 cups coconut. Pile into a 9-inch baked pie shell and top with remaining whipped cream. Sprinkle top with toasted coconut.

To toast coconut heat oven to 300°. Spread coconut in a cake pan, place in oven and turn the heat off. After 5 minutes take a peek. If lightly brown, remove and let cool. Store in a covered container.

A woman from Oslo, Norway, introduced herself as the head of the home economics department at the University of Oslo. She was touring the country to get ideas from outstanding restaurants to take back to Norway. I was happy and honored to give her my advice and a few of my favorite recipes.

French Cherry Cream Pie or French Blueberry Cream Pie

1 9-inch baked pie shell
1 3-oz. package cream cheese
1/2 cup powdered sugar
1/2 teaspoon vanilla extract
1 cup heavy cream, whipped
1 can cherry or blueberry pie filling

Cream the sugar, vanilla and cheese. Fold in whipped cream. Pour into the baked pie shell and put the cherry or blueberry pie filling on top. Chill several hours or overnight.

Strawberry Banana Cream Pie

1 9-inch baked pie shell
1 3.4-oz. package vanilla instant pudding & pie filling
1 1/4 cups cold milk
1 pint heavy cream, whipped
Bananas
1 cup sliced strawberries (more if you like)

Mix the pudding mix and milk together until stiff. Put in refrigerator while whipping the cream. Save about half the whipped cream for the top of the pie. Fold the whipped cream into the pudding mix.

Place sliced bananas on the bottom of a baked pie shell. Fold in some slices of bananas and sliced strawberries into the pudding mix. Pile into baked pie shell on top of sliced bananas. Top with remaining whipped cream. Store in refrigerator.

Toffee Cream Pie

1 9-inch baked pie shell
32 marshmallows
1/3 cup milk
6 Heath™ candy bar or chocolate covered toffee bar,
   chopped
1 cup heavy cream, whipped

Place the marshmallows and milk in the top of the double boiler. Stir in the Heath candy bars. When the marshmallows and candy have melted, remove from the heat and cool.

Fold in the whipped cream and pile into prepared pie crust. Refrigerate.

Comments

A fellow who wanted his eggs fried a certain way with cottage cheese went to great lengths to tell me just how to prepare the eggs. I knew there was no way I'd ever fix his eggs to suit him, so I said, "How about if I give you the pan, the eggs and whatever else you need, and you fix them?" He looked kind of surprised, got a little sheepish and said, "Oh, well, go ahead and fix them any way you want." I did and he went away happy – even though there wasn't a dab of cottage cheese anywhere close to his eggs.

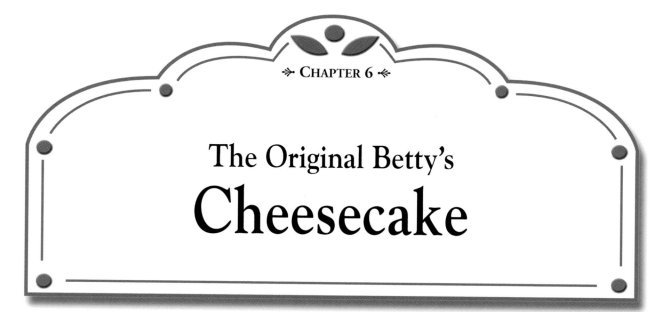

CHAPTER 6

The Original Betty's
Cheesecake

T he crumb crusts are the easiest of all to make, hold up especially well against moist fillings and don't get real hard when chilled. They work great for cream pies, ice cream pies and cheesecakes. Lately, I've been using low-fat crushed cinnamon graham crackers for my cheesecake crusts. The cinnamon is very mild, but adds a nice touch of flavor.

CHEESECAKE

Developing a Youth Market

Boys and girls would walk or bike the two miles from Two Harbors to go swimming in the Stewart River next to the cafe. When they finished swimming, they would stop in and I would sell them day-old cookies and brownies at a real bargain for their trek back to town. These kids really enjoyed the treats and would go home and tell their mothers about "Betty." Finally, the mothers began to come out to see who this Betty was! Since I'd grown up in Duluth and didn't know that many people in the community at the time, this was a great way to meet many local ladies.

The crew of Betty's Pies and some neighbors celebrate Betty's birthday in the early 1980s. During the summer, a large part of the staff was composed of college-aged students. In the early fall, when they went back to school, Betty's neighbors would offer to help at the restaurant.

Almond Cheesecake Pie

1/2 cup sliced almonds
1 9-inch prepared graham cracker or shortbread pie crust
1 3.4-oz. package cheesecake flavor instant pudding
 & pie filling
1 3.4-oz. package white chocolate flavor instant pudding
 & pie filling
1 1/4 cups cold milk (1% works fine)
1/4 teaspoon almond extract
2 cups heavy cream, whipped

Toast the sliced almonds in a frying pan over medium heat, stirring occasionally, about 7 minutes, until they begin to color and become fragrant. Immediately pour about half of them into the bottom of the prepared crust and put the rest into a dish to cool.

Meanwhile, in a medium bowl, combine the pudding mixes, milk, almond extract and half of the whipping cream. Beat with a wire whisk for 1 minute, or electric mixer on low speed. The mixture will be thick.

When the almonds in the crust are no longer hot, spread the pudding mixture over them. Whip 1 cup of cream and spread over the filling. Top with the remaining sliced almonds. Refrigerate.

We served a lot of cheesecake and I always tried to have it on hand, but we only really offered it in the classic form from the next recipe. Marti Sieber, one of the current owners, is a cheesecake fancier and we've now adapted several other recipes to tantalize cheesecake customers.

Betty's Cheesecake

1 graham cracker crust in a spring-form pan
4 eggs, separated
3/4 cup sugar
1/4 teaspoon salt
1/3 cup milk
1/2 cup cold water
2 Tablespoons unflavored gelatin
3 8-oz. packages cream cheese, softened
1/2 cup sugar
1 cup heavy cream, whipped
Graham cracker crumbs

This can either be put into a spring-form pan or 2 9-inch pie pans and served with a topping of cherry or blueberry pie filling.

Stir egg yolks, sugar, salt and milk in a double boiler over hot water until mixture thickens. Dissolve gelatin in 1/2 cup water. Add the 2 Tablespoons gelatin and work until smooth. Add the cream cheese and beat until well blended. Whip the egg whites until stiff and add 1/2 cup sugar. Fold this into the custard and cream cheese mixture.

Whip the cream and fold this into the mixture. Turn into the graham cracker crust. Top lightly with graham cracker crumbs. Refrigerate until served. This cheesecake freezes very well for longer storage.

It wasn't a Sunday, but 30 or 35 folks from a church congregation showed up at Betty's. Upon inquiring, I found out that their pastor had been in for lunch the previous week. Finding a line of people at the front door and down the driveway, he was about to leave, but was told that he'd better stay, because the pie was too good to miss. He must have agreed, because he told the congregation about us in his Sunday sermon. Result? A good many folks from his congregation came to find out for themselves – and left agreeing with him.

Mint Chocolate Chip Cheesecake

Crust
10 oz. graham cracker crumbs
2 Tablespoons sugar
1 teaspoon cinnamon
6 Tablespoons melted butter
1 teaspoon mint extract

Filling
4 3-oz. packages cream cheese, softened
1/2 cup sour cream, room temperature
2 1/2 cups sugar
4 eggs
1/2 cup heavy cream, room temperature
1 teaspoon peppermint extract
2 cups mint chocolate chips

Preheat oven to 350°.

Mix all crust ingredients and place in buttered spring-form pan. Chill while preparing filling.

Mix all ingredients in order, beating well after each addition until creamy. Do not overmix, since excess air will cause cheesecake to split. Turn into prepared crust. Bake in preheated 350° oven for 1 hour and 10 minutes or until golden. Cool in oven with door slightly ajar for 1 hour. Wrap in foil and chill at least overnight.

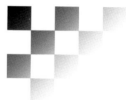

I've had pre-teen boys ask me, "Will you wait 'til I grow up 'cause I want to marry you?" It was all I could do to keep a straight face and reply, "I don't think my husband would like that very much!" I also remember a man who told me, "Hey, I'm going to leave my wife here and take you home with me." These kinds of proposals seem to reinforce the old saying that "the way to a man's heart is through his stomach."

Heath™ Bar Cheesecake

Crust

10 oz. vanilla wafers or graham crackers, crushed
2 Tablespoons sugar
1 teaspoon cinnamon
6 Tablespoons butter, melted
1 teaspoon vanilla extract

Filling

4 3-oz. packages cream cheese, softened
1/2 cup sour cream, room temperature
2 1/2 cups sugar
4 eggs
1/2 cup heavy cream, room temperature
1 teaspoon vanilla extract
1 2/3 cups toffee chips

Preheat oven to 350°.

Mix all crust ingredients and place in buttered spring-form pan. Chill while preparing filling.

Mix all ingredients in order, beating well after each addition until creamy. Pour into prepared crust. Bake in preheated 350° oven for 1 hour and 10 minutes. Cool in oven with door slightly ajar for 1 hour. Wrap in foil and refrigerate at least overnight.

Comments

One evening as we were getting ready to close, a woman came in, sat down and remarked, "I suppose you won't wait on me because I'm a Communist." I told her that I didn't care what she was and we'd be happy to serve her. She had a fresh trout dinner with Lemon Angel Pie for dessert. This woman was from Russia and had been on the French Riviera, where she met someone who told her that if she ever got to the shores of Lake Superior she had to be sure to stop at Betty's Pies. I sat and had a very nice visit with her – and we never even got close to talking about her politics.

Hazelnut Cheesecake

Crust

10 oz. vanilla wafers or graham crackers, crushed
2 Tablespoons sugar
6 Tablespoons butter, melted
1/2 cup toasted hazelnuts
1 teaspoon almond extract
1 teaspoon cinnamon

Filling

4 3-oz. packages cream cheese, softened
1/2 cup sour cream, room temperature
2 1/2 cups sugar
4 eggs
1/2 cup heavy cream, room temperature
1 teaspoon almond extract
3/4 cup coarsely chopped hazelnuts

Preheat oven to 350°.

Mix all crust ingredients and place in buttered spring-form pan. Chill while preparing filling.

Mix all ingredients until creamy. Do not overmix, since excess air will cause cheesecake to split. Turn into prepared crust. Bake in preheated 350° oven for 1 hour and 10 minutes or until golden. Cool in oven with door slightly ajar for 1 hour. Wrap in foil and refrigerate at least overnight.

The Original Betty's
Cookies & Bars

COOKIES

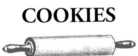

Continued

I have several different kinds of cookies in my freezer at all times. They're a good old standby and most freeze very well. When I bake a batch, I freeze half and put the rest in a tin or jar with a tight cover.

When mixing cookie dough, I never add all the flour called for. I hold out about 1/4 cup to see and feel the dough before adding more. Too much flour in a soft cookie will make it hard. And it's a good idea to bake off a cookie first before beginning to bake the whole batch.

I use butter in all my baking, but you can use half butter and half butter-flavored Crisco-brand shortening. If a recipe calls for sour milk or cream and you don't have any, put 1 teaspoon of vinegar or fresh lemon juice into a measuring cup and fill with milk. Let it stand a few minutes and it'll be ready for your recipe.

Be sure to preheat your oven to the correct temperature. When cookies are baked, remove them from the cookie sheet onto a rack to cool. Store in containers. For soft cookies, be sure to store them in a container with a tight fitting lid. If they dry out, add a piece of bread or apple, but replace the bread or apple often.

From Fish to Nuts

In the 1960s, the restaurant still had a meat case to hold smoked fish, fresh trout and other fish sales. Eventually, the case was removed.

BARS

I always line my cookie sheet with parchment paper, which saves having to grease the sheet. I usually press down cookies by placing waxed paper over the dough first, then pressing with the flat bottom of a glass. Some folks use the heel of their hand.

Bars make good snacks for young and old alike and they're so easy to make that it's a shame not to have them most of the time. Try not to overbake bars, or they'll get hard and dry. If underbaked, they are doughy, especially in the center. Bars are done when pressed slightly with a finger and a slight imprint remains or a toothpick inserted in the center comes out clean.

Cardamom Toast

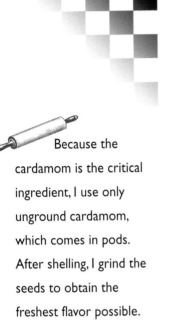

Because the cardamom is the critical ingredient, I use only unground cardamom, which comes in pods. After shelling, I grind the seeds to obtain the freshest flavor possible.

1 cup butter
1 cup sugar
2 eggs
1/3 cup half & half cream
1 teaspoon salt
18 cardamom seeds, crushed or 1 1/2 teaspoon ground
2 teaspoons baking powder
3 cups flour
1 egg white
water

Preheat oven to 350°.

Cream butter and sugar. Beat in eggs and cream. Sift dry ingredients together and beat into creamed mixture. On a lightly floured board make into 6 rolls and place on cookie sheet. Brush each roll with egg white mixed with 1 teaspoon water.

Bake 30 minutes at 350°. Remove from oven and slide onto a cutting board and slice diagonally. Put slices back on cookie sheet, cut side down, and return to oven to toast and brown. Check after 12 minutes and if lightly browned, turn over and bake 5 minutes more. Remove from oven and cool. Makes about 52 cookies.

Chocolate Chip Cookies

1 cup butter
1/2 cup packed brown sugar
1 cup granulated sugar
2 eggs
2 teaspoons vanilla extract
2 cups flour
1 teaspoon baking soda
1 teaspoon salt
2 cups semi-sweet chocolate chips
1 cup chopped walnuts

Preheat oven to 350°.

Cream the butter, brown sugar and white sugar. Beat in the eggs and vanilla.

Sift the flour, baking soda and salt together and beat into the creamed mixture. Stir in the chocolate chips and the chopped nuts by hand. Drop by teaspoonfuls onto a greased cookie sheet and bake for 10 to 12 minutes at 350°.

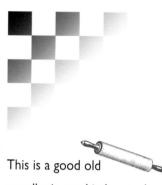

This is a good old standby in any kitchen and I always tried to keep them available. As sure as can be, if we ran out someone was sure to ask for them and be disappointed that we didn't have any.

Coconut Cookies

1 cup butter
1 cup packed brown sugar
1 egg
1 cup coconut, shredded
2 cups flour
1/2 teaspoon baking powder
1/2 teaspoon vanilla extract

Preheat oven to 350°.

In a medium bowl, cream the butter and brown sugar. Beat the egg and add with the coconut. Sift the flour together with the baking powder and add to the creamed mixture. Add the vanilla. Roll into 1-inch balls and place on a greased cookie sheet. Flatten with a fork. Bake at 350° for about 10 minutes.

This is an old recipe that was handed down to me by my great aunt. She always had them on hand when I visited her. They are simple to make and the brown sugar gives them a unique flavor.

Danish Dreams

1 cup butter
1 cup sugar
1 1/2 cups sifted all-purpose flour
1 teaspoon bakers ammonia*
1 teaspoon vanilla extract

Preheat oven to 325°.

Cream the butter and sugar together at high speed for up to 10 minutes.

Mix the flour and bakers ammonia together and add to creamed mixture. Add vanilla.

Drop on cookie sheet. Bake at 325° for 1/2 hour. This mixture can be put through a cookie press.

"Ammonia" as an ingredient in a recipe takes most non-Scandinavians by surprise, but believe me it's worth the search to find it and you can't make these cookies without it. The best place to look for it is in a Scandinavian grocery or food specialty store. In the Duluth area, the Scandinavian Designs and Tablewares store on East Superior Street carries the bakers ammonia needed here, as well as the vanilje sukker and pearl socker sugar called for in Drommer Swedish Cookies a bit later in this chapter. A final word on bakers ammonia: when you open the oven door, you'll be convinced by – I might as well say it – the "stink" that the cookies are ruined, but the odor quickly dissipates and the cookies are so light and wonderful that the smell will never bother you again.

Double Chocolate Cookies

This is NOT a light recipe, believe me! It's guaranteed to satisfy even the most extreme craving for chocolate.

2 1/4 cups flour
1 teaspoon baking soda
1 teaspoon salt
1 cup butter, softened
3/4 cup sugar
3/4 cup firmly packed brown sugar
1 teaspoon vanilla extract
2 eggs
4 1-oz. envelopes Choco-Bake™ unsweetened baking
   chocolate flavor
2 cups semi-sweet chocolate chips
1 cup chopped walnuts

Preheat oven to 375°.

   In medium bowl, combine flour, baking soda and salt; set aside. In large bowl, combine butter, sugar, brown sugar and vanilla; beat until creamy. Beat in eggs and Choc-Bake unsweetened baking chocolate flavor. Gradually beat in flour mixture. Stir in semi-sweet chocolate chips and nuts. Drop by rounded teaspoonfuls onto ungreased cookie sheet. Bake at 375° for 8 to 10 minutes. Cool completely on wire rack

Drommer Swedish Cookies

1/2 pound butter
1/3 cup vegetable oil
1 1/4 cups sugar
2 teaspoons vanilje sukker (Scandinavian vanilla sugar)*
1 teaspoon bakers ammonia*
2 1/2 cups flour (or a little more)

Topping
Pearl socker sugar*

This recipe was given to me by Darlene Johnson.

Preheat oven to 325°.

Mix the first six ingredients in the order given and chill dough for a short time.

Remove and roll into small balls. Dip tops in pearl socker sugar and press down lightly on the cookie sheet.

Bake at 325° for about 25 minutes.

* See earlier note under Danish Dream cookies on page 75 on these three ingredients.

Dutch Refrigerator Cookies

This was one of my mother's favorite old recipes and was always a treat for us kids when we were growing up.

1 cup butter
1/2 cup granulated sugar
1/2 cup packed brown sugar
1 egg
2 1/4 cups flour
1/2 teaspoon baking soda
1/2 teaspoon salt
1/4 teaspoon nutmeg
1/4 teaspoon cloves
2 teaspoons cinnamon
1 cup chopped walnuts

In a large mixing bowl, cream the butter and sugars. Add the egg and mix well. Sift the flour with the soda, salt, nutmeg, cloves and cinnamon. Add the egg mixture. Stir in the nuts and shape into rolls. Place in the refrigerator for 2 hours or overnight.

Heat oven to 375°. Slice cookies into 1/8-inch rounds and place on a greased cookie sheet. Bake 5 to 7 minutes.

Fruit Cookies

1 cup butter
1 1/2 cups packed brown sugar
2 eggs
1 1/2 cups flour
1 teaspoon salt
1 teaspoon cinnamon
1 teaspoon vanilla extract

1 cup flour
1 pound dates, chopped
4 slices colored pineapple, chopped
1 pound candied cherries, cut in half
1 cup whole filberts
1 cup pecans
1 cup walnuts

Preheat oven to 350°.

Cream the butter and brown sugar. Beat in the eggs. In a separate bowl, mix together the flour, salt and cinnamon. Beat in the vanilla.

Toss fruit in flour. Add flour-coated fruit to the batter. Mix by hand. Drop by teaspoonfuls onto greased cookie sheet.

Bake at 350° for about 15 minutes.

I make these in place of fruitcake for the holidays. They stay moist and are so easy to serve. Store in a covered container. They freeze well. Most important, they're so good you won't be wondering what to do with leftovers like fruitcake!

Orange Ginger Cookies

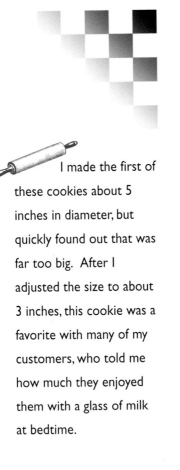

I made the first of these cookies about 5 inches in diameter, but quickly found out that was far too big. After I adjusted the size to about 3 inches, this cookie was a favorite with many of my customers, who told me how much they enjoyed them with a glass of milk at bedtime.

1 cup butter
1 1/2 cups sugar
1 egg
2 Tablespoons light corn syrup
1 Tablespoon freshly grated orange peel
2 3/4 cups sifted flour
2 teaspoons baking soda
2 teaspoons cinnamon
2 teaspoons ginger
1/2 teaspoon cloves

Preheat oven to 400°.

In a large bowl, cream the butter and sugar together. Beat in the egg, corn syrup and orange peel and mix well.

Sift the dry ingredients and add to the creamed mixture. Roll into balls about the size of a walnut and place on a greased cookie sheet.

Cover the balls on the cookie sheet with waxed paper and flatten with a glass.

Bake at 400° for 5 to 6 minutes.

Peanut Butter Balls

1 cup chunky peanut butter
2 Tablespoons butter, softened
1 cup powdered sugar
1/2 cup chopped nuts
2 cups Rice Krispies™

Wet your hands or put a little butter on them. In a medium bowl, mix all ingredients together by hand and roll into 1-inch balls.

Place on a cookie sheet and chill in the refrigerator.

Coating
1 cup semi-sweet chocolate chips
1 square unsweetened baking chocolate
1 square paraffin wax

In the top of a double boiler, place the chocolate chips, unsweetened baking chocolate and the paraffin wax. Melt this together. Keep warm while you dip the balls into the chocolate mixture.

Place on waxed paper. Put in refrigerator to set. When set, transfer to a bowl and store in the refrigerator.

We usually made these for our Christmas cookie assortment, but kids love them anytime. They add a nice variety to a cookie plate.

Potato Chip Cookies

These are a bit unusual, but I had a couple of customers from the Encampment Forest Association who liked these cookies so well they'd walk out if I was out of them when they stopped in for coffee.

1 cup butter
1 cup granulated sugar
1 egg
1 1/2 cups sifted flour
1 cup crushed potato chips
1/2 cup nuts, chopped
1 teaspoon vanilla extract

Preheat oven to 350°.

Cream the butter and sugar. Beat in the egg. Add the flour to the creamed mixture. Stir in the potato chips, nuts and vanilla. Roll the dough into 1-inch balls and place on a greased cookie sheet. Press down with a glass.

Bake in a 350° oven for 10 minutes or until lightly brown.

Snickerdoodles

9 Tablespoons butter (1 stick plus 1 Tablespoon),
   softened
3/4 cup sugar
1 egg
1/4 teaspoon salt
1 2/3 cups flour
3/4 teaspoon cream of tartar
1/2 teaspoon baking soda
1/3 cup sugar
4 teaspoons ground cinnamon

Preheat oven to 350°.

   In a large mixing bowl, cream the butter and sugar. Add the egg and mix well. Sift the dry ingredients together and mix with cream mixture. Roll dough in balls the size of a walnut. Mix sugar and cinnamon in a pie plate. Roll the balls in the cinnamon-sugar mixture.

   Place on ungreased cookie sheet, space 2 inches apart. Press down slightly with the bottom of a glass to 1/4 inch thick. Bake at 350° until cookies are golden at the edges, about 15 minutes.

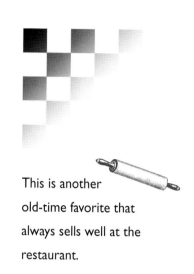

This is another old-time favorite that always sells well at the restaurant.

Sugar Cookies

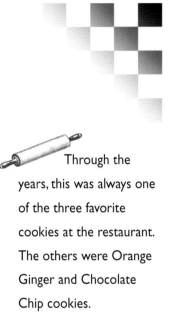

1 cup butter
1 cup granulated sugar
1 cup powdered sugar
2 eggs
4 cups flour
1 teaspoon cream of tartar
1 teaspoon salt
1 teaspoon baking soda
1 cup oil
1 teaspoon vanilla extract

Through the years, this was always one of the three favorite cookies at the restaurant. The others were Orange Ginger and Chocolate Chip cookies.

Preheat oven to 350°.

Cream butter with sugars. Add the 2 eggs and beat well. Sift the dry ingredients together and add to creamed mixture, alternating the dry ingredients with the cup of oil; add the vanilla.

Form into small balls and press down with a glass dipped in sugar for every cookie – or cover the cookie sheet with waxed paper and press the cookies down with a glass. Remove the waxed paper and sprinkle the cookies with sugar before placing them in the oven.

Bake at 350° for about 10 minutes.

Ting-A-Ling Cookies

2 4-oz. packages German's™ sweet chocolate
1 square unsweetened baking chocolate
2 1/2 cups Post Toasties™
1/2 cup shredded coconut
1/2 teaspoon vanilla extract

Melt the chocolate in the top of a double boiler; stir in the Post Toasties, coconut and vanilla.

Line a cookie sheet with waxed paper and drop the mixture by teaspoonfuls onto the cookie sheet. Place in the refrigerator to cool.

My brother and I always waited for our mother to make these. I think this was one of our favorites because it was like eating candy. About the only time she would make them would be for Christmas.

Vanilla Wafers

1 cup butter
2/3 cup sugar
2 teaspoons vanilla extract
1 teaspoon salt
2 eggs
2 1/2 cups sifted flour

Preheat oven to 375°.

Thoroughly cream together the butter and sugar. Add vanilla and salt. Add eggs, one at time, beating well after each addition. Stir in flour; mix well.

Drop by teaspoonfuls onto greased cookie sheet. Flatten with bottom of glass.

Bake in moderate 375° oven for 8 to 10 minutes, until edges are delicately browned. Remove immediately from cookie sheet. Makes about 6 dozen.

I used to bring these cookies to the nursing home while my friend June was there. They were a real favorite with her and the staff.

Wheaties™ Cookies

One of my customers would stop in the restaurant just to see if any of these cookies were in the jars. I would make them especially for him when I knew he would be in town.

1 cup butter
1 cup granulated sugar
1 cup packed brown sugar
2 eggs
2 cups shredded coconut
2 cups flour
1 teaspoon baking soda
1/2 teaspoon baking powder
1/2 teaspoon salt
1/2 teaspoon vanilla extract
2 cups Wheaties

Preheat oven to 350°.

Cream the butter and sugars together. Beat in the eggs one at a time. Beat in the coconut. Sift the flour, baking soda, baking powder and salt together and add to the creamed mixture. Add the vanilla and Wheaties. Drop by teaspoonfuls onto a greased cookie sheet and bake in a 350° oven for about 10 minutes. Don't overbake these cookies. If overbaked, they won't be chewy.

Brownies

1 cup butter
4 1-oz. bars unsweetened chocolate
4 eggs
2 cups sugar
1 Tablespoon vanilla extract
1 cup flour
1 teaspoon salt

Preheat oven to 350°.

Grease a 9-x-13-inch pan. In a small saucepan, melt the butter and chocolate together. In a medium bowl, beat the eggs, sugar and vanilla together. Add the melted butter and chocolate. Fold in the flour and salt by hand and spread into the greased pan. Bake 25 minutes at 350°.

Fudge Frosting
1 cup granulated sugar
1/4 cup butter
1/4 cup milk
1/2 cup semi-sweet chocolate chips
6 large marshmallows

Bring the sugar, butter and milk to a rolling boil. Remove from heat and add chocolate chips and marshmallows. Beat until creamy and spread over cooled bars.

This is an old standard and I made it about once a week, depending on my time. Brownies were not as important to have available as a good assortment of cookies and pies, so sometimes these got squeezed out during the busy season.

English Toffee Bars

This recipe came from a friend in Alabama and is really more of a home recipe than a restaurant item.

Club crackers
1 cup butter
1 cup packed brown sugar
2 cups (1 12-oz. package) milk chocolate chips
Ground nuts

Preheat oven to 350°.

Line jelly-roll pan with foil (a must to prevent sticking). Cover the bottom with club crackers.

Boil and stir butter and brown sugar together 3 minutes, being careful not to burn. Pour mixture over club crackers and bake at 350° for 8 minutes. Watch carefully so it doesn't burn. Remove from oven and sprinkle with milk chocolate chips, spreading to cover the baked mixture. Sprinkle ground nuts over top. Refrigerate 4 to 5 hours, then break into pieces. Store in cool place.

Kit Kat™ Bars

Club crackers
2 cups crushed graham crackers
2 sticks butter
1/3 cup granulated sugar
1 cup packed brown sugar
1/2 cup milk

Frosting
1/2 cup semi-sweet chocolate chips
1/2 cup butterscotch chips
2/3 cup peanut butter

All I can say about this and the next two recipes is: "Them is GOOD!"

Grease a 9-x-13-inch pan and line with club crackers (lay the crackers in one direction). Set aside.

Bring the butter, crushed graham crackers, sugars and milk to a boil and cook over low heat for 3 to 5 minutes.

Spread half of the cooked mixture over the crackers. Lay another layer of the club crackers on top and cover with the balance of the cooked mixture. Top with another layer of club crackers. Make sure the crackers all lay in the same direction.

Melt frosting ingredients in a double boiler. Spread over the top and refrigerate a few hours. Once set, separate into cracker-sized bars. Keep in the refrigerator.

O'Henry™ Bars

1 cup shortening
1 cup packed brown sugar
1/2 cup light corn syrup
4 cups instant (quick) oatmeal
Peanut butter (chunk style)
1 cup semi-sweet chocolate chips

Preheat oven to 350°.

Cream together the shortening and brown sugar. Beat in corn syrup, then mix in oatmeal. Blend and spread in ungreased 9-x-13-inch pan. Bake for 15 minutes at 350°, until edges start to bubble (it won't look done). Cool thoroughly.

Spread mixture with chunk style peanut butter. Sprinkle with the chocolate chips. Return the pan to the oven and leave until the chocolate chips melt. Spread like frosting. Let cool and harden in a cool place.

Toffee Bars

1 cup butter
1 cup packed brown sugar
2 cups flour
1 egg yolk
2 cups milk chocolate chips
Chopped nuts

Preheat oven to 350°.

Melt butter in a small saucepan. Take off the stove and add brown sugar, 1 cup of the flour, the egg yolk and then add the other cup of flour.

Pat this mixture into a greased 11-x-16-inch jelly-roll pan. Bake this at 350° for 15 to 20 minutes.

When the crust is done, remove from the oven and spread the milk chocolate chips on top. Spread and then sprinkle with chopped nuts.

Cut in diagonal pieces while still warm.

Another customer came in the front door and I greeted him. He said, "You're frying donuts and you're frying them in lard!" I asked how he could be so sure. "Because I can smell it," he said. "There's nothing better than donuts fried in lard!" I sold him donuts fresh from the fryer and he went on his way a happy man.

The Original Betty's
Breads & Quick Breads

Continued

There is something so tantalizing about homemade bread. I remember coming home from school as a little girl, opening the front door and the aroma of fresh-baked bread filling the house. My mother would cut off the crust for me and spread butter on it. The butter melted into the warm bread – ummm! It brings back such wonderful memories to me, even today, after baking thousands of loaves myself. I still make my own bread and rolls by hand, not yet a victim of a bread machine. I just like the feel of the dough and the kneading of it.

I use dry yeast, especially after my first experience with fresh yeast. After working very hard to set the bread and waiting hours for it to rise, I discovered I had killed the yeast by scalding it and had to start over again.

I've also been told stories by other women about working with fresh yeast. One I know to be a true story came from a friend who thought she had killed the yeast because her bread wasn't rising. She threw the whole batch in the garbage but, later, after the sun warmed up the garbage can, she was surprised to find that her dough had risen up and over the top and down the side of the garbage can. Even years later, she couldn't help laughing when she told the story.

Things are Always Rye at Betty's

Betty's Pies only served sandwiches one way – on Betty's Rye Bread. Baked fresh daily, it didn't last long. Cook Dianna Hood was expert at turning out delicious sandwiches.

When making muffins or quick breads, mix the batter as little as possible. The batter should actually have lumps in it. Pop the muffins into the oven as soon as you get the batter in the muffin tins. What can be better with your 10 a.m. coffee than fresh hot muffins?

Betty's Rye Bread

The first time I made this bread at home, I killed the yeast with the boiling water mixture. You could break windows with those loaves. My dad said, "Try again," and I got it right the next time and it was a staple all through the years.

2 1/2 to 3 Tablespoons dry yeast
1/2 cup warm water
1 Tablespoon sugar
4 cups medium rye flour
1 teaspoon baking soda
4 cups buttermilk

Dissolve the yeast in warm water with a Tablespoon of sugar. Set aside. Put rye flour into large mixing bowl, sprinkle baking soda over it and pour buttermilk on top.

1 1/2 cups water
3 Tablespoons shortening
1 cup packed brown sugar
2 Tablespoons salt
1/2 cup Grandma's Molasses
1 cup quick oats

2 cups bread flour
8 to 10 cups white flour

Combine water, shortening, brown sugar, salt and molasses in pan and bring to a boil. Add oats and cook for 5 minutes. Remove from heat and allow this mixture to cool, then pour it over the 4 cups of rye flour and add yeast mix. Mix well and add 2 cups bread flour. Add about 8 cups white flour, 2 cups at a time, to make a stiff dough. Take out of mixing bowl, place on a floured surface and knead in enough flour until dough is smooth and does not stick to surface – about 10 minutes.

Place in a greased bowl, cover and let rise until double in bulk. Punch down and shape into 5 loaves. Put in greased pans, prick with a fork or slash the tops about 3 times. Cover and let rise until slightly rounded over top of bread pans. Put the pans in a 350° preheated oven. Bake 30 to 35 minutes. When done, remove from oven and cool on a wire rack. Brush tops with melted butter to keep them soft. Makes 5 good size loaves.

Cardamom Coffee Cake

1 cake compressed yeast
1/4 cup warm water
1 teaspoon sugar
1 cup milk, heated
1/2 cup butter
1/2 cup sugar
1 teaspoon salt
1 1/2 teaspoons crushed cardamom seed*
4 egg yolks, beaten (reserve whites)
4 cups flour

Dissolve yeast in warm water with sugar. Add butter, sugar and salt to heated milk. Cool to lukewarm. Add yeast and cardamom. Mix well. Add beaten egg yolks. Blend in flour, mix well and place in a greased bowl. Cover and let rise for 2 hours. Turn out on floured board and shape into rolls or 2 braids. Let rise until double in size. Just before baking, brush with a beaten egg white mixed with a little water and sprinkle with sugar. Bake in a 350° oven for 25 to 30 minutes. Remove from pans and cool on a rack.

* See earlier note on cardamom seed under Cardamom Toast (page 72).

A man came in one day, ordered a sandwich, but said, "Huh … if your rye bread is like most, you can keep it. I don't want it." I told him I was sorry, but the rye was all we used for our sandwiches. "Well, then, give it to me," he said. I made his sandwich on my homemade rye bread and after he'd eaten every bit of it, he called me over and said, "That was the best rye bread I've ever tasted!"

Dilly Bread

This is a real light bread that has as much flavor as the ingredients would indicate.

1 Tablespoon yeast
1 teaspoon sugar
1/4 cup warm water
1 cup cottage cheese, lukewarm
2 Tablespoons sugar
1 Tablespoon onion juice
1 Tablespoon butter
2 teaspoons dill weed
1 teaspoon salt
1/4 teaspoon baking soda
1 egg
2 1/2 cups flour

Put the yeast and sugar into warm water. Combine the lukewarm cottage cheese, sugar, onion juice, butter, dill weed, salt and baking soda. Beat the egg and add along with the dissolved yeast. Mix in the 2 1/2 cups flour (may need a little more). Cover and let rise 60 minutes, punch down and shape into rolls or 1 loaf of bread. Bake at 350° for 20 minutes if rolls or 30 to 35 minutes if a loaf of bread. Brush with melted butter when taken from oven. Sprinkle with salt if desired.

White Bread

2 Tablespoons dry yeast
1/2 cup warm water
1 Tablespoon sugar
2 1/2 cups warm water
3 Tablespoons packed brown sugar
4 Tablespoons butter
4 teaspoons salt
2/3 cup instant potato flakes or buds
2 cups bread flour
4 1/2 cups white flour

Dissolve yeast in the 1/2 cup warm water with 1 Tablespoon sugar. Put the 2 1/2 cups warm water into a large mixing bowl and add the brown sugar, butter, salt, potato flakes and mix until butter is melted. (If you have water in which potatoes have been cooked, it makes an excellent substitute for plain warm water.) Add the 2 cups of bread flour and stir in the yeast mixture. Gradually add white flour to form a stiff dough. Knead on floured surface until smooth and satiny, 5 to 10 minutes. Place in greased bowl, turning dough to grease all sides. Cover with foil or damp towel. Let rise in warm place until light and doubled in volume, about 2 hours.

Punch down dough. Place on lightly floured surface and divide into 2 portions. Mold into balls. Cover again and let rise 15 minutes. Shape into loaves. Place in well-greased 9-x-5-x-3-inch pans, seam side down and cover with a towel. Let rise again in warm place until dough fills pans and tops of loaves are well above pan edges, about 1 1/2 hours. Bake at 350° for about 40 minutes, until golden brown. Remove from pans immediately; Brush with melted butter and cool on wire racks.

Makes 2 large loaves and 1 small one.

Whole Wheat Bread

2 cups milk
2 cups water
1/2 cup shortening
1/2 cup granulated sugar
1/2 cup packed brown sugar
1 Tablespoon salt
2 packages dry yeast
4 cups whole wheat flour
6 cups white flour

Heat the milk and water to lukewarm. Add the shortening. Mix in sugars and salt to liquid.

In a separate cup, dissolve 2 packs dry yeast in 1/2 cup warm water with 1 Tablespoon sugar.

In large mixing bowl put 4 cups whole wheat flour and pour the warm mixture over it. Add the yeast that has been dissolved. Add 6 to 7 cups white flour to make a stiff dough. Cover and let rise until double in size. Punch down and shape into 4 loaves.

Place in greased bread pans and let rise until just above the pans. Bake at 350° about 40 minutes. Remove and cool on racks.

Comments

One day in Duluth, I pulled into a filling station to gas up my car. A man at the pump ahead of me looked at my license plate, which says, "Pielady." He said, "You have to be Betty from Betty's Pies, if you've got the nerve to drive around with that license plate." All I could do was laugh and agree with him. They call these licenses "vanity plates," but I like to think there's more than just vanity involved in this case.

Continued

Banana Chocolate Chip Pecan Bread

1/2 cup butter, softened
1 cup sugar
1 large egg
1 teaspoon vanilla extract
1 cup mashed ripe bananas (about 3)
3 Tablespoons milk
2 cups flour
1 teaspoon baking powder
1/2 teaspoon baking soda
1 cup semi-sweet chocolate chips (or mini chips)
1/2 cup pecans, chopped

In a large bowl, cream together butter and sugar. Add egg and vanilla, mix until fluffy. Set aside.

In small bowl, mix bananas and milk and set aside.

In another bowl mix flour, baking powder and baking soda. Add dry ingredients alternately with banana-milk mixture to creamed butter mixture, beating until blended. Stir in chips and pecans by hand.

Spoon batter into greased and floured loaf pan. Bake in preheated 350° oven for about 1 hour or until knife inserted in center comes out clean. Do not overbake, as bread will become dry. Cool in pan 10 minutes, take out of pan and cool completely on a rack.

As an alternative, in place of chips and pecans, add almonds, almond extract and white chocolate chips.

Each of the thousands of customers we served through the years voted for Betty's Pies by pulling off the busy highway into a tiny parking lot, standing in line, when necessary, to buy and pay for our goodies and in almost every case left as completely satisfied patrons. In claiming the title of "Pielady," I like to think that my customers awarded it to me – because I earned it.

Carrot Bread

This is another recipe I love and really get hungry for, but it's not on my diet so all I can do is want it!

2 cups flour
2 teaspoons baking soda
2 teaspoons cinnamon
1/2 teaspoon salt
1 1/2 cups sugar
2 cups grated raw carrots
1/2 cup currants or raisins
1/2 cup coconut
1/2 cup chopped pecans
3 eggs
1 cup vegetable oil
2 teaspoons vanilla extract

Mix flour, baking soda, cinnamon, salt and sugar together. Add carrots, currants, coconut and nuts. In a separate bowl, beat eggs and add oil and vanilla. Add first ingredients to liquid mixture and mix well. Pour into 3 greased 7 1/2-x-4-inch loaf pans. Let stand 20 minutes. Bake in a 350° oven for 45 minutes to 1 hour or until a toothpick inserted in the center comes out clean. Cool slightly and remove from pans. When cool, wrap and refrigerate.

Cherry Nut Bread

1/2 cup butter
1 1/2 cups sugar
3 eggs beaten
1 teaspoon vanilla extract
2 1/2 cups flour
2 teaspoons baking powder
1/4 cup cherry juice
1/2 cup milk
1/2 cup cherries, cut up
1 cup chopped nuts

This is a colorful sweet bread that looks especially nice in an assortment.

Cream the butter and sugar; add beaten eggs and vanilla. Sift the flour and baking powder together and add to the butter mixture alternately with the milk and cherry juice. Stir in the cherries and nuts.

Pour into greased 9-x-5-inch loaf pan and bake for 1 hour at 325° or until toothpick inserted in middle comes out clean.

Remove from pans and cool.

Chocolate Zucchini Bread

Here, at last, is the perfect way to use up all that zucchini that gardeners love to produce.

2 1/2 cups flour
1/2 cup cocoa powder
2 1/2 teaspoons baking powder
1 1/2 teaspoons baking soda
1/2 teaspoon salt
1 teaspoon cinnamon
3/4 cup butter
2 cups sugar
3 eggs
2 teaspoons vanilla extract
2 cups grated zucchini
1/2 cup milk
1 cup chopped nuts

Sift dry ingredients together. In a mixing bowl, cream the butter and sugar. In a separate bowl, mix together the eggs, vanilla, zucchini, milk and nuts. Alternate combining the zucchini mixture and dry ingredients with the creamed mixture. Spread batter into 2 greased loaf pans. Bake at 350° for 1 hour. Cool.

Donuts

1 cup sugar
3/4 cup sour cream
1/4 cup buttermilk
3 eggs beaten
1 teaspoon baking soda
1 teaspoon baking powder
1/2 teaspoon nutmeg
1/2 teaspoon salt
3 1/2 cups flour

In large mixing bowl, mix the sugar, sour cream and buttermilk. Mix well and let sit about 5 minutes. Beat the eggs and add to the sugar mixture. Sift the dry ingredients together and add to the mixture and blend. Place in a covered bowl and put in the refrigerator overnight. Roll out and cut with donut cutter, then fry in hot lard. Makes about 30 donuts.

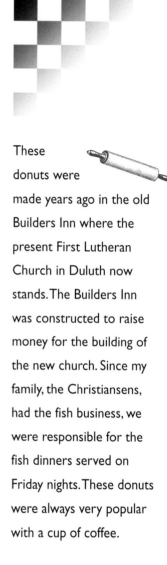

These donuts were made years ago in the old Builders Inn where the present First Lutheran Church in Duluth now stands. The Builders Inn was constructed to raise money for the building of the new church. Since my family, the Christiansens, had the fish business, we were responsible for the fish dinners served on Friday nights. These donuts were always very popular with a cup of coffee.

Easy Pull-Apart Breakfast Bread

3/4 cup pecans, chopped
18 frozen Parkerhouse-style rolls
1/2 cup butter, melted
1/2 cup packed brown sugar
1 teaspoon cinnamon
1 3-oz. package vanilla pudding (not instant)

Generously butter a Bundt™ or tube pan and sprinkle with chopped pecans. Stack and arrange frozen rolls evenly in pan. Mix melted butter, brown sugar, cinnamon and powdered vanilla pudding mix together. Pour mixture over frozen rolls. Cover with a tea towel and let stand at room temperature overnight.

In the morning, bake rolls in a preheated 350° oven for 25 minutes. Cool in pan for 10 minutes, then invert on a plate and serve by pulling rolls apart.

A home economics teacher in Duluth gave me this recipe. I like it because it is really simple and easy – and it was always a good morning item on our menu.

Giant Popovers

6 Tablespoons butter, melted
6 large eggs
2 cups milk
2 cups flour
1 teaspoon salt

Preheat oven to 375°.

Prepare popover batter about 1 1/2 hours before serving.

Grease eight (8) 2 1/2-inch-deep custard cups well. Set cups in jelly-roll pan for easier handling.

In small saucepan, melt butter. In large bowl, with mixer at low speed, beat eggs until frothy. Beat in milk and butter until blended. Beat in flour and salt until smooth.

Fill each custard cup 3/4 full with batter. Bake 1 hour then quickly make a small slit in top of each popover to let out steam; bake 10 minutes longer. Immediately remove popovers from cups. Serve hot.

Traditionally, we always served these popovers with our baked fish dinners. They are especially good with fruity jams or jellies like strawberry, pin cherry or marmalade.

Lemon Loaf

1 cup margarine
2 cups sugar
4 eggs
Grated rind of 2 lemons
3 cups flour
2 teaspoons baking powder
Pinch of salt
1 cup milk
Nuts, if desired

Topping
Juice of 2 lemons
1/2 cup sugar

Cream the margarine and sugar. Beat in eggs one at a time. Beat in lemon rind. Sift flour, baking powder and salt together and add alternately with the milk.

Bake in 2 loaf pans at 350° for 1 hour. When done, mix juice of 2 lemons and 1/2 cup sugar together. Then spoon mixture over top of bread while still hot.

Morning Glory Muffins

2 cups flour
1 1/3 cups sugar
1 teaspoon cinnamon
1/2 teaspoon nutmeg
1/4 teaspoon salt
2 teaspoons baking soda
1 cup vegetable oil
2 teaspoons vanilla extract
3 eggs
2 cups carrots, grated
1 apple, grated
1/2 cup raisins or dates
1 cup nuts, chopped
1/2 cup coconut

Mix the dry ingredients; add oil, vanilla and eggs. Don't overmix. Then add remaining ingredients and blend. Fill greased muffin tins almost full. Bake 20 minutes in a 350° oven. Makes 2 dozen.

I always tried to have these muffins available because they sold so well on coffee breaks.

Orange Cranberry Muffins

1 1/2 cups flour
1/2 cup whole wheat flour
2 teaspoons baking powder
1 teaspoon baking soda
1 teaspoon salt
1/2 teaspoon cinnamon
1 medium seedless orange unpeeled
1 cup fresh or frozen (not thawed) cranberries
2 large eggs
1 cup applesauce
1 cup packed brown sugar
3 Tablespoons chopped walnuts

Preheat oven to 400°.

Lightly coat a 12-cup muffin tin with vegetable oil cooking spray.

In a large bowl, sift together the dry ingredients, set aside. Scrub the outside of the orange, cut it into eight sections, place in a food processor and puree. Add the cranberries and pulse until coarsely chopped. Add eggs, applesauce and brown sugar and pulse until mixed. Pour into flour mixture, and stir just until blended.

Spoon into the muffin cups. Sprinkle with walnuts. Bake 18 to 20 minutes or until the tops spring back when lightly touched. Remove muffins from pan and cool on wire rack.

Poppy Seed Bread

2 eggs
1 cup sugar
1 cup vegetable oil
1 cup evaporated milk
2 cups flour
2 teaspoons baking powder
1/2 teaspoon salt
1 teaspoon vanilla extract
1/4 cup poppy seeds

Beat eggs and add the sugar. Stir in the cooking oil and evaporated milk.

Sift the flour, salt and baking powder together and add to the egg mixture. Stir in vanilla and poppy seeds.

Pour into a 9-x-5-inch greased loaf pan and bake for 1 hour at 350°. Remove and cool.

My friend June was into antiques and I went to Chicago with her to do the big antique show at the Arlington Race Track. We were sitting in the booth and a woman walked by, turned around, looked at me for a few seconds and said, "What are you doing here? You belong back in the pie shop, not sitting here in an antique show." It seems that I met customers everywhere I went and I still do today.

Pumpkin Bread

2 cups pumpkin
4 eggs
1 cup vegetable oil
1/3 cup water
3 1/2 cups flour
3 cups sugar
1 Tablespoon pumpkin pie spice
2 teaspoons baking soda
1 1/2 teaspoons salt

Combine pumpkin, eggs, oil and water; mix well. Sift together remaining ingredients. Add pumpkin mixture; mix well. Pour into 2 greased and floured 9-x-5-inch inch loaf pans.

Bake at 350° for 1 hour and 10 minutes or until done. Remove and cool. Nuts may be added.

Rich Shortcake

2 cups flour
3 teaspoons baking powder
1/2 teaspoon salt
2 Tablespoons sugar
1/2 cup butter
1/2 cup half & half
1 egg, beaten

Preheat oven to 450°.

Sift dry ingredients into mixing bowl. Cut in the butter with fork or pastry cutter. Mix half & half and egg together. Lightly mix this into the dry ingredients just enough to moisten.

Drop onto an ungreased cookie sheet and bake for 8 to 10 minutes. Makes 6 to 8.

This is an outstanding shortcake on which to put fresh strawberries or other fruit toppings.

Scones

We never served scones when I had the restaurant, but they are now a good item there and I like to make them for my own use.

4 cups flour
1/4 cup baking powder
1/2 cup sugar
2 sticks butter (1 cup)
6 eggs
1 cup buttermilk
1 1/4 cups raisins

Preheat oven to 400°.

Sift first three ingredients into a large mixing bowl. Mix in butter until sandy in texture. Mix eggs and buttermilk thoroughly then add mixture to bowl. Add raisins and mix, but don't overwork the dough or it will be tough. Roll dough out 1 inch thick and cut out small circles or squares.

Place on greased cookie sheet and bake at 400° for about 20 minutes. Makes about 50 pieces.

Sopapillas

2 cups flour
2 teaspoons baking powder
1 teaspoon salt
2 Tablespoons lard
2/3 cup warm water

In a medium size mixing bowl put the 2 cups flour, baking powder and salt. Cut the lard into the dry ingredients. Sprinkle 1 Tablespoon of water over mixture at a time, tossing lightly. Gather dough into a ball. Cover and refrigerate for 30 minutes.

Heat 2 inches of oil to 400°. Roll dough on lightly floured board into rectangle. Cut into strips 3-by-2 inches. Fry in deep fat 3 or 4 at a time. Turn only once – fry about 2 minutes. Remove from pan with a slotted spoon and drain on paper towels. Serve hot with honey. Make a slit in them to put the honey in.

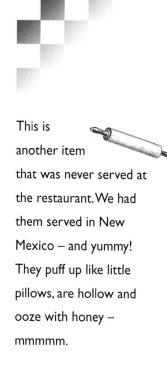

This is another item that was never served at the restaurant. We had them served in New Mexico – and yummy! They puff up like little pillows, are hollow and ooze with honey – mmmmm.

113

Swedish Toscakake

1/2 cup butter
2/3 cup sugar
2 eggs
2/3 cup flour
1 teaspoon baking powder
2 Tablespoons milk

This is great to serve friends for a coffee break. A Swedish woman gave me this recipe. She always served it when folks dropped in.

Preheat oven to 350°.

Line bottom and sides of a 9-inch heavy skillet with foil. Cream butter and sugar together. Add eggs one at a time, beating 1 minute after each addition. Blend in half of the dry ingredients then add 2 Tablespoons of milk and the remaining dry ingredients. Blend thoroughly at slow speed. Spread into heavy skillet and bake at 350° for 25 to 30 minutes. During the last 5 minutes of baking time, prepare the topping (below) and spread over the warm cake and put under broiler for 1 to 2 minutes.

Topping
1/4 cup butter
1/4 cup sugar
2 Tablespoons flour
1 Tablespoon cream

Mix and cook in saucepan over medium heat stirring constantly until mixture comes to a boil. Spread on hot cake and sprinkle with 1/3 cup slivered almonds.

Broil for 1 to 2 minutes.

The Original Betty's
Index

Ingredients Index

History Index

The Original Betty
About the Author

I AM BETTY

Betty Lessard, the "Pielady," spent 28 years in the kitchen of her restaurant, serving hundreds of thousands of customers and trying to ensure that every one of them left the establishment satisfied that they had enjoyed the best baked goods on earth.

Now retired, Betty lives on the shore of Lake Superior near the Stewart River, within sight of the new Betty's Pies restaurant. Her three schnauzers are active company on daily walks. Her large collection of rolling pins reminds her that she is, indeed, The Pielady.

For a catalog of
the entire
Lake Superior
Port Cities
collection of books
and merchandise,
write or call:

**Lake Superior
Port Cities Inc.**
P.O. Box 16417
Duluth, MN 55816

Outlet Store:
310 E. Superior St. #125
Duluth, MN 55802

1-888-BIG LAKE
(888-244-5253)
218-722-5002
FAX 218-722-4096

www.lakesuperior.com
E-mail: *guide@lakesuperior.com*

Also from Lake Superior Port Cities Inc.

Lake Superior Magazine (Bimonthly)

Lake Superior Travel Guide (Annual)

Hugh E. Bishop:

The Night the Fitz Went Down
Softcover: ISBN 978-0-942235-37-1

**By Water and Rail: A History of
Lake County, Minnesota**
Hardcover: ISBN 978-0-942235-48-7
Softcover: ISBN 978-0-942235-42-5

Haunted Lake Superior
Softcover: ISBN 978-0-942235-55-5

Haunted Minnesota
Softcover: ISBN 978-0-942235-71-5

**Lake Superior, The Ultimate
Guide to the Region**
Softcover: ISBN 978-0-942235-66-1

Bonnie Dahl:

Superior Way, Third Edition
Softcover: ISBN 978-0-942235-49-4

Joy Morgan Dey, Nikki Johnson:

Agate: What Good Is a Moose?
Softcover: ISBN 978-0-942235-73-9

Daniel R. Fountain:

**Michigan Gold,
Mining in the Upper Peninsula**
Softcover: ISBN 978-0-942235-15-9

Marvin G. Lamppa:

Minnesota's Iron Country
Softcover: ISBN 978-0-942235-56-2

Daniel Lenihan:

**Shipwrecks of Isle Royale
National Park**
Softcover: ISBN 978-0-942235-18-0

Betty Lessard:

Betty's Pies Favorite Recipes
Softcover: ISBN 978-0-942235-50-0

James R. Marshall:

**Shipwrecks of Lake Superior,
Second Edition**
Softcover: ISBN 978-0-942235-67-8

**Lake Superior Journal:
Views from the Bridge**
Softcover: ISBN 978-0-942235-40-1

Howard Sivertson:

**Schooners, Skiffs & Steamships:
Stories along Lake Superior
Water Trails**
Hardcover: ISBN 978-0-942235-51-7

Tales of the Old North Shore
Hardcover: ISBN 978-0-942235-29-6

The Illustrated Voyageur
Hardcover: ISBN 978-0-942235-43-2

**Once Upon an Isle:
The Story of Fishing Families
on Isle Royale**
Hardcover: ISBN 978-0-962436-93-2

Frederick Stonehouse:

**Wreck Ashore: United States
Life-Saving Service, Legendary
Heroes of the Great Lakes**
Softcover: ISBN 978-0-942235-58-6

Shipwreck of the Mesquite
Softcover: ISBN 978-0-942235-10-4

Haunted Lakes (the original)
Softcover: ISBN 978-0-942235-30-2

Haunted Lakes II
Softcover: ISBN 978-0-942235-39-5

Haunted Lake Michigan
Softcover: ISBN 978-0-942235-72-2

Haunted Lake Huron
Softcover: ISBN 978-0-942235-79-1

Julius F. Wolff Jr.:

**Julius F. Wolff Jr.'s
Lake Superior Shipwrecks**
Hardcover: ISBN 978-0-942235-02-9
Softcover: ISBN 978-0-942235-01-2